Wing Chun Kung-fu: A Complete Guide

VOLUME ONE

Basic Forms and Principles

CHINESE MARTIAL ARTS LIBRARY

WING CHUN KUNG-FU

VOLUME ONE

Basic Forms & Principles

Dr. Joseph Wayne Smith

CHARLES E. TUTTLE CO., INC.
Rutland, Vermont & Tokyo, Japan

Disclaimer
Please note that the publisher of this instructional book is
NOT RESPONSIBLE in any manner whatsoever for any injury that may result
from practicing the techniques and/or following the instructions given
within. Since the physical activities described herein may be too
strenuous in nature for some readers to engage in safely,
it is essential that a physician be consulted prior to training.

Published by the Charles E. Tuttle Publishing Co., Inc.
of Rutland, Vermont & Tokyo, Japan
with editorial offices at
1-2-6 Suido, Bunkyo-ku, Tokyo 112

LCC Card No. 92-80688
ISBN 0-8048-1718-9

First edition, 1992
Second printing, 1992

Printed in Japan

Contents

Introduction

This book is the first in a series of three volumes that collectively give a theoretical overview as well as practical instructions for the entire system of Wing Chun kung-fu. There are many Wing Chun books on the market today, and the addition of more requires justification. First, Wing Chun today is not a homogeneous phenomenon: there are various types of Wing Chun/Wing Tsun in Hong Kong based on the style of Yip Man, many American and Southeast Asian forms of Wing Chun, and at least three forms of Wing Chun in mainland China. In this book, I cautiously wish to stay away from the internal disputes between these schools. It is sufficient to say that each of these styles has its strengths and weaknesses.

Saying that there is a best style is like saying that there is a best gun—however, it is well-known that handguns, shotguns, semi-automatics, and machine guns all have their advantages and disadvantages. For example, a handgun is for close-range work and is easily concealed, whereas a carbine and shotgun are not easily concealed without sawing off the barrel, which reduces power. However, the carbine and shotgun are typically more powerful than the handgun (*see* T. Lesce, *Shootout II: More Techniques of Modern Gunfighting* [Phoenix, Arizona: Desert Publications, 1981]).

The same thing can be said about martial-arts styles and sub-styles. My approach is a synthetic one: not to mix together an eclectic bag of randomly selected techniques, but to systematically unify and integrate a diverse array of martial-arts knowledge into a concise and functional whole that is both meaningful and practical. The resulting theory of Wing Chun, while obviously in debt to historical systems of Wing Chun, is a rational reconstruction that is an expression of my own understanding and beliefs.

In addition, the approach I have taken toward martial-arts knowledge and teaching gives priority to scientific analysis rather than to history and tradition. While I am a teacher of a classical system, I approach it in a non-classical way. Scientific analysis, when conducted properly, emphasizes rationality, logic, justification, and criticism. It is also honest, meaning that the limits and weaknesses of the approach are clearly stated, not hidden from discussion.

In the first volume, *Basic Forms and Principles*, I shall discuss and illustrate in full the three empty-hand forms of Wing Chun kung-fu: *Sil Lum Tao, Chum Kil*, and *Bil Jee*; in the second volume, *Fighting and Grappling*, I shall describe sticky-fighting and grappling techniques, as well as the concept of vital points; and in the third volume, *Weapons and Advanced Techniques*, I shall describe the wooden-dummy set, the use of butterfly knives and other weapons, and advanced techniques of Wing Chun.

In each of these books I hope to present a scientific approach to the martial arts, explaining why techniques work and also when they will not work. Further, I hope to be able to do this without undue technicalities, so that this material is readable and concise, and illustrated with photographs that are meaningful.

In the light of the above comments, it goes almost without saying that I have no wish to enter into political disputes about what is the real *Sil Lum Tao, Chum Kil,* and *Bil Jee,* who is a real master, what is the authentic style of Wing Chun (or Wing Tsun), and so on. These political questions have no part in a truly scientific study of the martial arts; consequently I do not claim to present here the sacred Truth about Wing Chun as revealed to me by God! The scientific method and the true martial-arts spirit are both conducive to humility and selflessness; I therefore give thanks and homage to all of my teachers and the masters of their lineages, and hope that these works are free of the vice of self-promotion and serve to enrich the science and art of Wing Chun kung-fu.

1

The *Sil Lum Tao* Form and *Chi Kung*

INTRODUCTION

In this chapter, I shall illustrate and fully explain the meaning of the first form of the Wing Chun system, the *Sil Lum Tao,* or Small Thought form. *Sil Lum Tao* is the best known, and perhaps most important, form in the Wing Chun system. It is also the form that causes the most confusion among students. Indeed, some of the errors made in misinterpreting *Sil Lum Tao* may lead a student to almost certain defeat against a good street fighter. So let me proceed immediately to clear up the confusion. In these three volumes, I hope to place Wing Chun kung-fu on a coherent and scientific foundation, as well as to defend my style against many critics who see it as impractical, illogical, and fundamentally nonviable as a combative art. I shall attempt to show that Wing Chun is a very valuable fighting style, that is practical, economical, and logical.

Writers of books on Wing Chun constantly praise their style as being a logical one, but they never go beyond mere assertion and attempt to justify this by showing how and why the techniques work.

THE THEORY OF THE CENTER-LINE STANCES

Classical Wing Chun kung-fu is typically defined by means of what is known as the center-line theory, which is the foundation of the system, determining both the fighting stance and the logic of combat. The center-line is taken to be an imaginary line that passes through the median axis of the body. It is on this axis that the most vulnerable organs of the body are located. The fighter therefore defends this area by keeping his elbows in the center-line or plane of the body in both attack and defense and seeks to attack the center-line of the opponent. Wing Chun attacks must typically be linear because of the requirement of keeping the elbows in the center-line; in addition, the shortest distance in space between two points (such as a knuckle and a nose), is a straight line, so linear attacks are much faster than circular roundhouse style swings. It is also more difficult to defend against straight-line attacks because they are direct, fast, and tend not to inform the opponent of the intent to attack.

So far so good; all of this is true. However, there is a tendency for Wing Chun practitioners to fight front-on in a *Chil Ying* position. The fighter stands in a parallel stance known as *Kim Nur Mar*. This is the well-known, pigeon-toed, foot-adducted Wing Chun stance—the knees and toes point in toward the median axis of the body, with there being no more than a fist's distance between the knees. Some Wing Chun fighters stand in a much wider stance, suitable for riding goats, and have up to four or five fist widths of space between the knees. There are a number of things scientifically wrong with using the parallel stance, or *Kim Nur Mar,* as a fighting stance, which I now summarize:

a) It exposes the maximum surface area of your body to your opponent, at least 25% more area than the side-on stance preferred by *Jeet Kune Do* fighters, boxers, and Thai kick-boxers.

b) The old-time champion boxer Len Harvey said that balance is the key to successful fighting (Len Harvey, *Modern Boxing.* [London: Blackie and Son, Ltd., 1937], p. 11). Balance governs advancing, retreating, footwork to the left and right, and checking attacks. The *Kim Nur Mar,* or parallel stance, is not stable from the front (or back), its stability is from the side (try it with a friend who pushes you). Yet by facing your opponent head-on, you are presenting your unbalanced side. The parallel stance is more stable than standing up straight, but this is only because by bending your knees you lower your center of gravity. Compare the stability of the Wing Chun parallel stance to the side with the normal stance for boxing and note the difference for yourself.

c) The parallel stance simply doesn't allow meaningful footwork. If there is no footwork, then there can be no victory.

d) It is well known to boxers and kick-boxers that the back hand or the back foot is the power hand or foot. The reason for this is that in kicking or punching with the back foot or hand there is a natural transfer of body weight into the attack. Fighting in the *Chil Ying* position doesn't effectively allow this; it doesn't allow for explosiveness of attack.

e) The large gap between the knees makes the fighter vulnerable to Wing Chun's sticky-leg or *chi gerk* attacks (*see* the second volume in this series, *Fighting and Grappling*) as well as to front kicks to the groin.

Thus, I believe that the parallel stance should be used in Wing Chun as a training stance only. The knees are locked together while you perform the hand movements of *Sil Lum Tao*, to place strong isometric tension upon the leg muscles, thereby strengthening the legs for sticky-leg fighting. The correct fighting stance of Wing Chun, *Som Kwok Bo*, comes from the second form of Wing Chun, the *Chum Kil*, or Searching for the Bridge set, and is a side-on position with the forward foot turned slightly in and the back foot held at 45 degrees to the median axis of the body. The feet are customarily placed about a shoulder's distance apart, but you should employ it with no more than a fist's width between the knees when you are actually engaged in close-range fighting. The reason for this is technical and depends upon a knowledge of sticky-leg fighting. Approximately 70% of the fighter's body weight rests on the rear foot, and 30% on the forward foot.

When using the side-on fighting position described above in an actual fighting situation, the Wing Chun fighter does not necessarily attack through the center-line by passing through the median axis of his own body. The attack is made through a center-line that runs down from the practitioner's eyes, through the front defensive hand (which is held up high in order to guard the head), and through the forward leg. This is a powerful and directed line of attack that is aligned to the median axis of the opponent's body. However, for close-range or street fighting, I prefer to use the *Chil Ying* position for the upper body, with the legs held as described above.

Attack ideally involves breaking through your opponent's guard and then attacking his poorly protected side, locking up his leg in order to control his ability (or breaking the knee with a sticky-leg technique), controlling his hands with sticky-hand movements, and then attacking his vital points. Moving into an opponent and getting control of his side puts him at a disadvantage, for now there are two hands against his one. He is effectively fighting two opponents, or fighting at half-strength!

THE STRUCTURE OF THE *SIL LUM TAO* FORM

The *Sil Lum Tao* form is performed in a stationary parallel stance and involves only hand movements. It consists of an opening sequence and three sections. As it would be far too boring to describe every hand move verbally, it is better to consult the photographs. What I shall do however, is to discuss some of the least understood Wing Chun hand movements, as well as some of the better known ones that are often misused.

THE OPENING OF THE *SIL LUM TAO* FORM
AND PUNCHING THEORY

The version of the *Sil Lum Tao* form given here does not begin with the fists placed beside the chest. The form opens with *til sao*, a defensive movement involving an upward lift of the arm, palms facing the body with fingers open, followed by a sudden lateral jerk of the wrist and the grasping formation of a claw hand, with its withdrawal to beside the chest. The *til sao*, or lifting deflection, is especially designed for counter-attacking a punch with a grappling hand move. There is a detailed theory of grappling, or *chin-na*, in Wing Chun that I shall discuss in the second volume of this series. For the moment, I want to point out that the *til sao* block has merit as a defensive hand move in that it can successfully defend a wide area of the upper body from hand attacks.

The formation of the claw hand and a twisting grab—as if to tear flesh from the bones of an opponent—is a technique constantly found in all three empty-hand forms of the Wing Chun system. The self-defense techniques using the claw, which I shall detail in volume two, are extremely brutal and must only be used in life-or-death situations. These include: gouging out the eyes, ripping out the hair by the roots, dislocating the jaw, tearing the flesh of the nose, ears, and lips, crushing the throat, and twisting and ripping the testicles. Such clawing techniques are a very effective means of self-defense for women finding themselves in violent rape attacks.

There are four open-handed strikes in Wing Chun kung-fu. The chop is a strike delivered with the blade of the hand. It is delivered with a snap of the arm to generate impulse—the sudden release of force in a very short time interval. The palm strike is a short-range linear attack which uses the heel of the hand. Force is generated by exploding with the body weight behind the strike, using the arm much like a battering ram. The side palm strike is similar to the palm strike but the target is the opponent's side. There is a slight curve in the path of the attacking hand which impacts again on the heel of the hand, the force however is generated by a snapping action of the wrist. The cutting side palm generates its force by snapping the wrist, like the side palm. However the surface of impact is smaller, being the small round bone on the heel of the hand. The striking angle is the same as the side palm but it can also be used as an overhead strike to the face.

The most important hand move in the opening of the *Sil Lum Tao* form is the vertical punch. This punch is designed for close range combat. The vertical fist-thrusting punch in the form is executed by sliding the forearm across the chest with the fist pointing across the body. The fist is then pointed toward an (imaginary) opponent and delivered so that any punching attack initiated by the opponent will meet the bridge arm (forearm) and be blocked. Even if the punch is not a successful strike, once contact with the opponent's arm occurs, the sticky-hand fighting skills can be employed.

Wing Chun punches typically involve inch-force, or *ging*, an explosive shock-wave effect. There is a lot of mystical nonsense written about the one-inch punch that knowledge of physics readily dispels. The idea behind snap punching is to reduce the time in which the fist is in contact with the body. This increases the impulse (the product of the average magnitude of a force on a body and the time for which it acts.) The great old-time boxer Tommy Burns said that the most feared punch is not a big swing or a long straight drive out from the shoulder, but "one of those half-arm jabs, which only travel about a foot or at most 18 inches, and which have the full weight of the shoulder behind them" (T. Burns, *Scientific Boxing and Self Defence,* London: Athletic Publications Ltd., 1934, p. 31).

Wing Chun punching also is greatly aided by exploding one's body weight behind a punch. Jack Dempsey in his *Championship Fighting* (Long Beach, CA: Centreline Press, 1978) described a method of power punching involving a falling step, where a punch is launched after putting your weight on the front foot and then stepping and punching so that gravity gives a great momentum to a punch. However, Dempsey's falling step occurs quite naturally after either a back-foot or front-foot heel kick, because as the foot comes down, the body starts to fall. A coordinated punch delivered at this time can have knock-out power. Other ways of putting body weight behind a punch include springing or leaping forward to bridge the gap with a jab and surging upward, using the legs as springs to fire a lifting punch or upper cut.

The vertical fist has been criticized on the grounds that there is a lack of bone support for the fifth metacarpal bone. However, in Wing Chun, we don't land blows on the little pinky knuckle, but on the bottom three knuckles, which do give solid bone-to-bone contact for the transmission of impact force. It may be of interest to note that the great Jack Dempsey favored a vertical punch (*see Championship Fighting* ibid.), as did other old-time boxing champions such as Robert Fitzsimmons (*Physical Culture and Self-Defense,* London: Gale and Polden, Ltd., 1902, Chap. 18) and Jim Driscoll (*Text-Book of Boxing,* London: Athletic Publications, n.d.).

THE FIRST SECTION OF THE *SIL LUM TAO* AND *CHI KUNG* TRAINING

The first section of the *Sil Lum Tao* is done very slowly for the purpose of *Chi Kung* (Pinyin: *qigong)* training as well as for isometric tension exercises for the wrist and forearm, to improve the strength of the *taun sao* and *fook sao*. The internal *taun sao* (finger-drop, palm-twisted *taun sao*, or asking hand) is a straight thrusting-hand move used to deflect punches. Wing Chun is a very economical style: hard blocking is not desirable because re-direction of force is safer, quicker, and less demanding on your health and energy. The internal *taun sao* is used in close-range fighting, much like a punch: it moves along the body and then outward to catch any punching attack and harmlessly redirect it. A correct *taun sao* has the elbow in the center of the body, at solar plexus height. The palm faces upward, fingers straight and piercing forward to the eyes, in the case of the conventional *taun sao*, or else the wrist is twisted and the index finger is straight with the other fingers raised. This latter *taun sao* is designed for sticky-hands, and thus it sticks better to an opponent's forearm. In any case, a good *taun sao* has an angle slightly greater than 90 degrees between the biceps muscle and forearm. Any less and the *taun sao* is too weak; any more and punches will skate over the top of it.

The hand moves of the *haun sao* and *jut sao* and *wu sao* (defensive hand) techniques are discussed later. The *fook sao* hand movement, however, is quite often puzzling to students, so it is worthwhile to take a closer look at its meaning and use. The *taun sao* and *fook sao* techniques are two important hand moves of Wing Chun's sticky-hand style, occurring in both single and double sticky-hands (*chi sao*). The *fook sao*, or hooking (lying-on-top) hand, consists of the hand bent at the wrist so that the fingers face in toward the median axis of the body. The shape of the fingers is dictated by the need of this hand move to lock up the *taun sao* in sticky-hands. Like the *taun sao*, a good *fook sao* consists of the elbow in the center-line and not merely the wrist, preventing the passage of the thrusting *taun sao* not by virtue of the wrist action, but because the forearm blocks its passage. The *fook sao* is typically used, along with pivoting and footwork, to redirect attacks. In particular the *fook sao* is a quasi-grappling hand. In many cases it is far too slow to attack an opponent by grasping an opponent's arm. Instead, one may use the *fook sao* to hook down the guard and attack. Thus, while the *fook sao* is at first glance an unusual hand move, its usefulness is obvious.

There are two hand moves in the opening of the *Sil Lum Tao* that merit a brief comment before I discuss *Chi Kung*. These moves are the downward X-hand and the cross-hand movement. The former move is not identical to the X-block usually found in karate. In Wing Chun, we do not use two hands to do what one hand could do, because in the case of a double lower block, one's head is now vulnerable to attack. Nor would we attempt to perform hard blocking against a kick—Wing Chun is a soft/hard form of kung-fu believing that defense should be soft, involving deflection and flowing with the attacking force, while offense should be hard, directing the hard attacking weapons of the body against the weak points of human anatomy. The X-hand is a classical hand move, merely used to judge the center-line of the body when in the parallel stance.

The cross-hand movements are performed immediately after the opening punch in the *Sil Lum Tao,* consisting of an upward, downward, leftward, and rightward movement of the wrist. This is done not only to train the flexibility of the wrist, but because it embodies an important technique that is fully utilized at the *Bil Jee* level. The fingertips in *Bil Jee* fighting are often used to attack around a block or defense by being flicked around it. The cross-hand movement represents the various angles of a flicking finger attack; this movement, like all other offensive hand moves, should involve inch-force, or *ging.*

For traditional Chinese kung-fu and other internal arts, the union of physical energy, breath (*chi*), and spirit is the highest aim of training. When this is done the five elements—metal, earth, water, fire, and wood—are in balance. *Chi Kung* is a way of obtaining the inner harmony of the body and spirit. This is a vast topic that cannot be adequately addressed here. However, I will summarize here a *Chi Kung* exercise that is practiced in the *Sil Lum Tao.* Grip the ground strongly with your toes to unite yourself, according to tradition, with the earth. Relax the body, close your eyes and concentrate on the *tan-t'ien* (lower abdomen). The tongue touches the roof of the mouth in breathing in, said by the Chinese to connect the major channels of *chi*-energy circulation. Inhale slowly expanding the *tan-t'ien;* exhale slowly, relaxing the *tan-t'ien.*

While this concentrated breathing occurs, a series of exercises are performed for the *pubococcygeus* muscle (PC), similar to the exercises now known as the Kegel exercises. The PC muscle controls urine flow and its spasmodic contractions constitute orgasm. Contract and release this muscle—squeeze it as tight as possible for 10 seconds, release, and then squeeze again and so on. A strong PC muscle prevents sagging of the pelvic organs, and can increase the intensity of the orgasm. Dr. Arnold Kegel devised a series of exercises for the PC muscle in the late 1940s, but Wing Chun practitioners interested in *Chi Kung* have been training this muscle for at least three thousand years!

THE SECOND AND THIRD SECTIONS
OF THE *SIL LUM TAO*

The second and third sections of the *Sil Lum Tao* are very straightforward and are described by the captions to the photographs in this chapter. The palm strikes, chops, and finger thrusts are self-explanatory offensive weapons, or, in the case of the side palm, *pak sao*, a defensive parry. The second and third sections of the *Sil Lum Tao* also contain techniques for force redirection. The double lifting hands and the drawing-in are primarily used in close-range fighting to disrupt the flow of energy of an opponent's attack. The drawing-in hand movement involves having both of your hands on the outside of your opponent's hand. This is a strongly disadvantageous position as the median axis of your body can be readily attacked. The drawing together of an opponent's hands constitutes a hand trap and puts you in the advantageous position. The drawing-down hand (*la*) and the upward-lifting wrist movement (*ding*) in the third section of the *Sil Lum Tao* are not primarily used as blocks, but rather function in sticky-hand fighting as conventional ways of opening up an opponent's guard by either moving the guard down or up, followed by an immediate attack. The *haun sao* and *jut sao* from section one of the *Sil Lum Tao* also serve a similar purpose. The *jut sao* is a sudden downward jerk with the edge of the heel of the hand, to clear a pathway for a strike. The *haun sao* is a wrist-rotating movement, used to twist around guards, or to open up a guard. In both cases we can see the evidence of the concept of sticky-hands; the use of all these hand moves presupposes that contact has already been made with the opponent's hands, or forearms.

The *bong sao* hand movement is one of the most important hand movements in Wing Chun, but it is also the most complex and least understood. There are many types of *bong sao* movements in Wing

Chun, including the wooden-dummy section, but to keep this discussion concise and uncluttered I will consider here only the simple *bong sao* in the *Sil Lum Tao*. The *bong sao* consists of a bent-elbow hand formation, such that the blade of the hand faces upward. The angle of the elbow is slightly greater than 90 degrees: any less and the hand movement is too weak, any more and punches will skate over the top. The elbow is elevated so that the shoulder is blocked from view of the attacker. This means that a punch will be deflected upward and will not be long enough to connect. The *bong sao,* therefore, functions as a distance-destroying deflection. The hand is bent for the purpose of sticky-hands, so as to glue to an opponent's hand. This means that your hand is already inside an opponent's guard, which wouldn't be the case if all you did was raise your elbow to defend yourself. All that now needs to be done to counter-attack is to straighten the elbow to launch a *bil jee* to the throat, or alternatively to rotate the hand in order to drop a back fist on the opponent's nose.

The *bong sao,* like all hand moves, has its weaknesses. It is weak to the side if an opponent pushes your elbow in toward your chest, and most importantly it is weak in the respect that it leaves your side unguarded. That is why in sticky-hands, the hand sequence goes from *bong sao* to *taun sao*—the Wing Chun hand moves are a coherent system of internally related hand moves that shift from one to another to cover up possible weaknesses in the preceding hand move. My system, like Western boxing, therefore places great emphasis upon combinations, not only attacking combinations but defensive ones as well. I cannot emphasize strongly enough how important in fighting it is to develop fast, fluid, and clear combinations, because unless you are fighting a fool, no fight against a skilled opponent can be ended by just one master technique. There is always the possibility in the heat of combat that your best technique may not work as it worked while sparring in class. Therefore, a good fighter is versatile, capable of both defending from all angles and attacking from all angles. Indeed, the ideal is to not merely simultaneously defend and attack with a hand or leg move, but to simultaneously defend and attack an opponent with both a hand technique and a sticky-leg technique with follow-ups. In the next chapter I shall begin describing how this is possible with a description of the Wing Chun footwork at the *Chum Kil* level.

1

THE *SIL LUM TAO* FORM AND *CHI KUNG*

OPENING

1. To perform the first form of Wing Chun Kung-fu, the *Sil Lum Tao,* or Way of the Small Thought, stand in the attention position, with your back straight, eyes focused straight ahead upon the horizon, your feet together, and your hands at your sides. In performing the Wing Chun forms, emphasis is placed upon symmetry: the left-hand movements and the right-hand movements are performed as if there were a mirror running through the center-line of the body. For this reason, to make matters clearer, hand techniques are often shown here only on the left-hand side, because the right-hand techniques are exactly the same but performed on the right. In this photograph, the center-line is an imaginary line

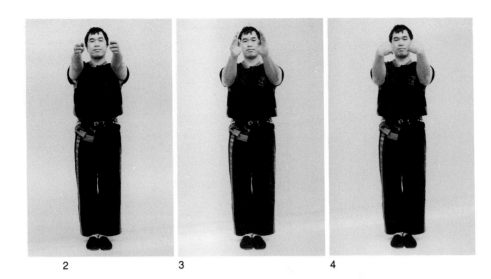

2   3   4

running through points in the middle of the subject's body. Maintain deep but relaxed breathing throughout the form.

2. Now move both hands slowly upward to perform a double *til sao,* or upward lateral wrist deflection. Both hands are moved together, at a deliberately slow pace, with the thumbs of both hands facing up, the knife edge of your hands facing downward. Slowly move your hands until your arms are fully extended and at right angles to your body. The fingers and wrists are very relaxed, like the leaves of a willow tree.

3. Perform the double *til sao.* This defensive hand move is an upward deflection of a straight punch in which you should attempt to get under the punch, stick to the opponent's hand, and grapple. In the form, the actual *til sao* movement is the sudden snap of the wrist. While the hand movements were previously slow, relaxed, and deliberate, the *til sao* is rapid and sudden, like the lightning-like strike of a coiled snake (one of the animal symbols of the Wing Chun system). This part of the form is designed to train your wrist muscles.

4. With your arms fully extended at right angles from your body, turn both hands through a 360-degree rotation, the left hand turning clockwise, the right hand turning counter-clockwise. Turn very slowly and concentrate on tensing the muscles in your wrists to perform a dynamic tension exercise. (This is a resistance exercise for muscles, using the body's own muscles as isometric resistance.) Spend at least a few minutes on this strengthening exercise, with the rest of your body in the attention position.

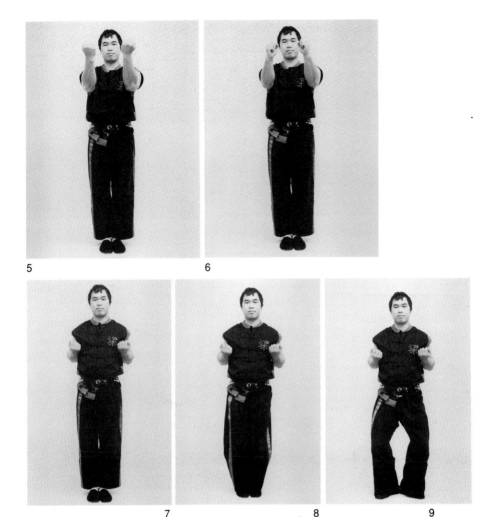

5

6

7

8

9

5–6. Complete the wrist rotation (left hand clockwise, right hand counter-clockwise), or *haun sao* (5) so that the extended fists are in the basic Wing Chun sun fist position, that is, with the hands in a closed fist, with both thumbs facing up (6).

7. Now withdraw your fists rapidly to the attention position, this time holding them to either side of your chest, both arms bent and thrust backward in order to stretch the chest muscles.

8. Bend your knees about 120 degrees.

9. Now turn your toes out, the heels of both feet still remaining together. The angle defined by this arc is approximately the same as the angle of your bent legs.

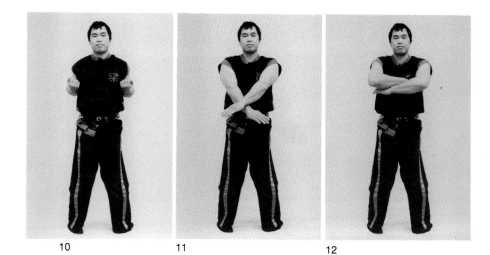

10   11   12

10.   From this position, in one fluid movement, turn your toes inward and your heels out. Lock your knees together to form the basic Wing Chun training stance (different from the fighting stance). The knees are bent as previously described, and the toes are turned in. For beginners, keep the distance between the knees about two to three fist widths, but later, as you become accustomed to the position, sink deeper into the stance by allowing your knees to come together, and lock them in this position. This is a dynamic tension exercise for the legs. Grip the floor with your toes in order to apply further tension to your legs. At advanced stages, *Chi Kung* breathing is practiced along with various tension exercises for other muscles.

11.   The form now proceeds by swiftly thrusting down into a low cross-hands. Note that the left arm is on top of the right arm.

12–13.   Draw your hands up, so that your hands rub along your stomach and lower chest with your elbows held as close as possible to the center-line of the body (12). This is to train you in the skill of close internal hand movements for very close-range fighting. The arms move upward until the upper segment of your arm is a right angle to your body. Your hands scrape across your chest in performing this rising circular movement, and a double back fist is delivered with a great concentration of power (13). This part of the form trains you in delivering a powerful close-range attack within a small fighting circle.

Having completed this technique, withdraw hands to the basic attention position shown in Figure 10.

13   14   15

16   17   18

14.   From the basic attention position, place your left fist in your center-line, such that the distance between your wrist and your chest is approximately one-and-a-half times the distance from your knuckles to your wrist.

15.   Deliver a left center-line punch. When the arm is fully extended, leave it in that position, with your hand held in the Wing Chun sun fist, the thumb facing upward.

16–24.   Now perform a set of hand movements known as the snake-hand or cross-hand movement, with the extended left hand. The sequence is done as follows: bring the hand up, with fingers up (16); bring your hand down, with fingers down (17); move it to the

SIL LUM TAO AND *CHI KUNG* • **23**

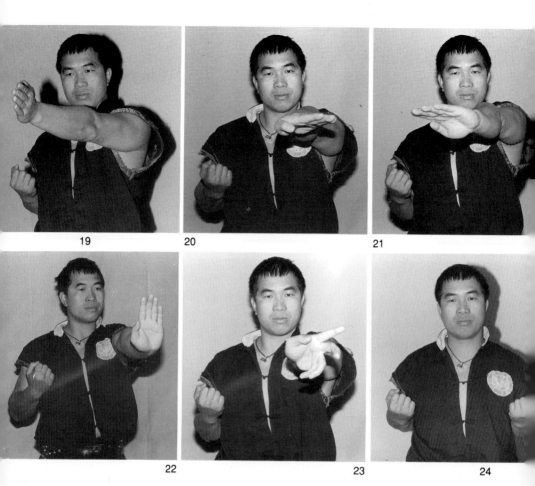

19   20   21

22   23   24

left (18) and to the right (19); turn your hand over, palm facing down, then turn your hand to the left (20); then perform the same movement to the right (21); turn your hand so that the palm is vertical (22); form a claw-hand, tensing the fingers (23); from the claw-hand, form a fist and immediately withdraw your left fist back to the Wing Chun attention position (24). The purpose of this exercise is to develop wrist flexibility, although at advanced levels it can be incorporated into other basic-fighting hand moves, involving a flicking attack of the fingers, from the *Bil Jee* form.

From the attention position, now put your right fist in your center-line, a fist-and-a-half's distance from your chest, and repeat all of the movements given above (16–24) using your right hand. The snake-hand, or cross-hand, is performed with

25   26   27

any left flick of the wrist being performed before a right flick of the wrist. When the right hand has been withdrawn to the attention position, the opening of the *Sil Lum Tao* form has been completed.

SECTION 1

25. This section begins with the left hand sliding across the chest slowly, with the fingers straight and the palm up. The movement stops when the left bicep is tucked firmly against the chest.

26–27. A sudden lifting or jerking move of the wrist and fingers forms the *taun sao,* or asking-hand (26). In close-range fighting, it would constitute a close-to-the-body scooping deflection of a straight punch, and the movement of the arm from the close-to-the-body position to full extension (27) would be swift. In the form, the movement is deliberately slow, for the purpose of dynamic tension. Thrust your fingers through your central plane toward an imaginary opponent with intense concentration of your arm muscles. The completed *taun sao* consists of the extended arm in your center-line, the angle between the forearm and the biceps slightly greater than 90 degrees; your arm should be strongly resistant to pushing, for the aim of the *taun sao* is to stick onto an opponent's arm. This is why the fingers are turned up—to lock onto an opponent's arm—and the wrist is twisted slightly off center while the index finger is fully extended, which naturally raises the other fingers. In *chi sao,* or sticky-hands, this maximizes the contact surface, and hence the control over an opponent's arm.

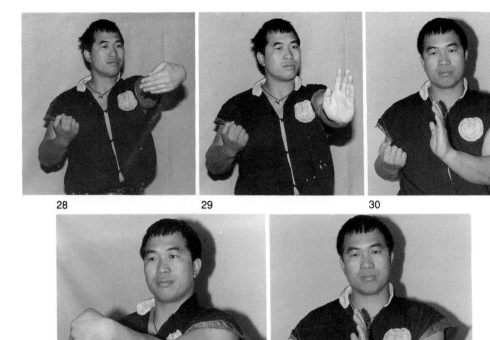

28 29 30

31 32

28. From the extended *taun sao,* perform a *haun sao,* or a clockwise 360-degree turn of the wrist, ending at a hand formation with the wrist bent and the fingers held straight, pointing upward.

29. You have now formed the *wu sao,* or defensive hand, and its formation is known as worshiping the Buddha, since the shape of the hand resembles a hand held in prayer.

30. The *wu sao,* or defensive hand, is slowly moved back toward one's body until reaching a distance of about a fist-and-a- half's width from your chest.

31. Now drop your hand to form the *fook sao,* or hooking deflective hand (this is only a description of the movement). The wrist is bent and held in the center-line, and the palm faces toward the chest. Move your *fook sao* slowly out though your center-line until your arm is extended such that the angle between your upper arm (biceps) and forearm is about 140 degrees.

32. Perform the *haun sao,* or clockwise rotation of the wrist, until the hand is back in the *wu sao* position. Repeat the movements (28–

33

34

35

31) two more times. You have now worshiped the Buddha three times. The ancient Chinese believed that three was a lucky number and based the system around this number and triangles.

Having done this, remain with your arm extended and your hand in the *wu sao* position.

33.   Deliver a side palm strike.

34.   Deliver a palm strike through your center-line, then perform a *haun sao,* or hand rotation, and form the Wing Chun fist.

35.   Withdraw your arm and return to the basic attention position.

> **Repeat the above sequence (25–35) on the right-hand side, beginning with the right asking-hand, or *taun sao,* going to the final palm strikes with your right hand, first to the left, and then through your center-line. Perform the *haun sao*, or hand rotation, and then form the Wing Chun fist. Withdraw your arm and return to the basic attention position. This completes the first section of the *Sil Lum Tao* form.**

37   38

36

39   40   41

SECTION 2

36. The second section of the *Sil Lum Tao* begins with rapid movements, in contrast to the first section of the form. Perform double palm strikes first in front of you, then directly to your sides, and then behind you. Sometimes the form is abbreviated by performing only the front palm strikes and then moving on to the double bar arm position, as shown here.

37. Form the double bar arm, left arm upon right arm, your upper arm at 90 degrees to your trunk. This hand move is used as a double-arm block to defend the chest and face.

38. From the double bar arm position, perform a double chop.

39. Return now to the double bar arm position, this time with the right arm on top of the left arm.

42   43

44   45

40.   From that position, deliver a double downward chop.

41.   From the bottom of the chop, turn your hands over, palms up, and quickly jerk your hands up until they are in the position shown in the photograph. The form is often simplified by deleting this movement and performing a double *taun sao* after the chop.

42.   Now bring your arms back close to your chest, ready for a double *bil jee,* or finger thrust, to an imaginary opponent's eyes.

43.   Perform the double *bil jee* to the imaginary opponent's eyes.

44.   Drop your hands in a double palm strike (*la*) in front of you.

45.   Raise both arms and execute a double wrist block, or upward lifting wrist movement (*ding*).

Withdraw the hands and return to the basic attention position to complete the second section of the *Sil Lum Tao* form.

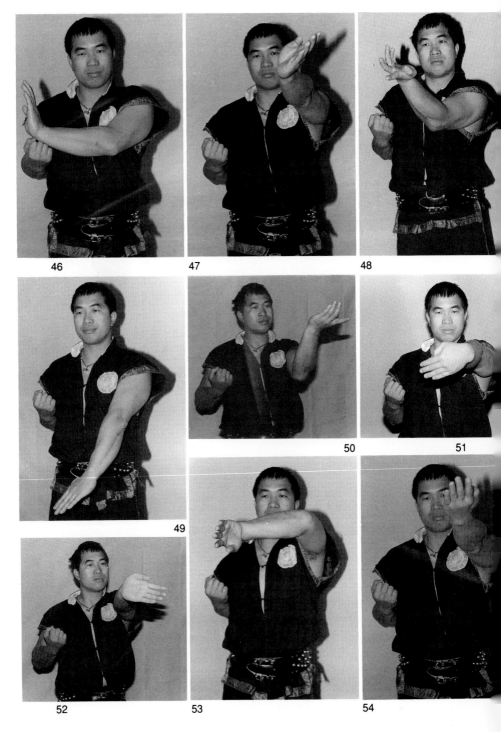

46   47   48

49

50   51

52   53   54

SECTION 3

46. The third section of the *Sil Lum Tao* form begins with the execution of a left palm strike at 45 degrees to your body.

47. From the furthest extension of the arm from the 45-degree palm strike, flip your arm back into your center-line and for an instant perform a *taun sao* as illustrated in Figure 27.

Then, from that position, deliver a cutting side palm to the throat as shown here. Form the Wing Chun fist, as described in Figure 15, and withdraw your left arm back to the basic attention position.

Now repeat the movements above (46–47) with your right arm.

48. Swiftly perform a left *taun sao,* thrusting your defensive hand through your center-line.

49. Deliver a downward chop from the *taun sao* position; this is known as a *gaun sao.*

50. Return now to the *taun sao* position.

51. Perform the *haun sao,* or clockwise wrist rotation, until your left hand is held, as depicted in Figure 52, with your fingers to the left, palm facing the opponent.

52. Deliver a side palm strike and return to the attention position.

Now repeat the movements above (48–52) with your right arm.

53. Perform a left *bong sao,* or wing-arm deflection. Notice that the correct *bong sao* position has the elbow higher than the wrist, so that punches do not sail over the forearm. The purpose of this defense is to enable a straight punch to be deflected by an upward force, so that sticky-hands, (*chi sao*) and grappling (*chin-na*) may be used.

54. Drop your elbow into your center-line in order to form a *taun sao.* The *taun sao* shown in this photograph is an elementary *taun sao* that is only moderately good for sticking onto an attacking arm, but certainly more than adequate for deflecting straight punches.

55 56 57

58 59

55. From the *taun sao,* perform a palm strike, with your fingers facing down. This illustrates the basic types of palm strikes, each suitable for a specific situation and angle of attack.

Withdraw your left arm and return to the basic attention position. Then repeat all these movements exactly on the right-hand side, concluding once more with your body in the basic attention position.

56. Deliver a low *bil jee,* or finger thrust, with your left hand, to an imaginary opponent's groin.

57. Place your right arm on your left upper forearm, while your left arm is still fully extended in the low *bil jee* position. Cut your right

60

hand down your left forearm as if strapping a razor or sharpening a knife. At the last instant, thrust your fingers into an imaginary opponent's groin. Keep the right arm extended.

58. Repeat this cutting hand movement, this time cutting with the left hand, and make a finger thrust with the right hand.

59. Deliver three Wing Chun punches—left, right, and left.

60. Closing of the form: after the last punch, withdraw your arms to the basic attention position. Move your heels in together, and then your toes. Straighten your legs. This is the reverse of the opening of the *Sil Lum Tao* form. Standing with your feet together, slowly move your hands down by your sides in depressing side palm strikes, while exhaling.

This completes the *Sil Lum Tao* form.

2

The *Chum Kil* Form and Footwork

INTRODUCTION

In the previous chapter, I described the Wing Chun fighting stance and outlined precisely what is wrong with fighting in the parallel stance. In this chapter, I shall discuss the theory and meaning of the *Chum Kil* or bridging the gap form and the philosophy of combat espoused by Wing Chun. I shall also discuss the subtle meaning of selected hand movements in the *Chum Kil* form, outlining their relevance to combat.

THE *CHUM KIL* FORM AND FOOTWORK

As can be gathered from Chapter 1, Wing Chun's stance makes it a small-circle, close-range system. This fact can also be ascertained by considering Wing Chun's footwork. The system involves two forms of walking—heel-walking and toe-walking. Heel-walking involves simply stepping forward with the front foot and dragging up the back foot. This type of footwork is not preferred for very close range attacks, but is usually used to bridge the gap. The toe-walking footwork involves lightly lifting the heel of the front foot and pushing forward on the toes. This footwork is designed for very close-range sticky-leg fighting. This footwork is designed for a specific purpose and is not invalidated by the fact that in other combat situations a longer form of footwork is necessary. In kick-boxing and tournament fighting where higher kicks are required, the *Muay Thai* or Western boxing footwork is excellent.

However, all that needs to be done to reach a boxing stance from the free-fighting stance of the *Chum Kil* is to rise up. To go from a boxing stance to the close-range *Chum Kil* stance, all that is necessary is to sink the knees and close the gap between the legs. In the second book in this series I shall describe how one can integrate and unify Wing Chun and Thai boxing.

Footwork, as any good boxer or kick-boxer will tell you, is important for generating knock-out power in punches and kicks. In Wing Chun, the theory is the same: attacking power is developed by exploding the body weight into a kick or a punch. This idea is best seen in the case of punching. A back-foot heel kick, even if it may not reach the opponent, puts the body into motion and bridges the gap. A lead punch will have extra power because of the falling body weight. I shall discuss ways of bridging the gap in the next section; for the moment let me re-emphasize the important connection between footwork and kicking and punching power.

Good footwork enables sudden and rapid changes in your body position in relation to the constantly changing stimuli of combat. A.T. Slater-Hammel ("Initial Body Position and Total Body Reaction Time," *Research Quarterly* **24**:91–96 [1953]) investigated the effect of initial body position or stance upon total body reaction time. The variation in stance involved the variables of body weight and the position of the knees. The starting positions were: a) knees straight with weight distributed over the feet; b) knees straight with weight on the balls of the feet; c) knees bent with weight distributed over the feet; d) knees bent with weight on the balls of the feet.

It was found that while for each weight distribution group, no significant differences were found for starting reactions involving the position of the knees, the starting positions with the body weight distributed over the feet were significantly shorter than those positions with the weight over the balls of the feet. It was concluded that starting reactions from the balls of the feet required more time because of the time required to lower the heels to the floor. I conclude that the theory of Wing Chun's footwork is consistent with Slater-Hammel's study and his conclusion about fast footwork.

FOOTWORK, BRIDGING THE GAP,
AND FIGHTING STRATEGIES

Good techniques are of little use unless you can successfully bridge the gap between yourself and your opponent. By successfully, I mean hitting him without getting caught by him in the process. There are three basic concepts central to successfully bridging the gap: timing, tempo, and rhythm. Timing is the skill of defending or attacking at just the right instant when an opponent is open. In particular, the most skillful aspect of timing is to set up and deceive your opponent so that you catch him coming in, so that he walks right into a punch or kick. This sort of strategy can maximize the destructive force of your attack because the total force that penetrates your opponent is the vectorial sum of his forward force, plus your own attack, launched with your full body weight behind it. This analysis therefore suggests one way in which the gap can be bridged—by counter-fighting, allowing your opponent to bridge the gap himself, while with cunning and precise timing you attack straight through his opening. Whatever technique is used against you will leave an opening if by precise timing and footwork you can make your opponent miss, and it is by correct timing that you make the most of these opportunities. This skill can only be obtained by the hard sweat and pain of sparring.

The second concept, tempo, refers to the speed at which a fighter attacks or defends, while rhythm is the spatio-temporal organization of attack and defense—the pace of the fight. The speed of your opponent and the pace of the fight itself also suggest ways of bridging the gap. Against a faster opponent, you must fake techniques in the hope that he responds and opens up. Against a slower opponent it may be preferable to simply beat him to the attack, hitting him before he can hit you. In addition to this another somewhat brutal way of opening up an opponent is to attack his weapons. Punch or kick the arms or legs, so that his guard drops and/or his footwork slows, and then work your attacks into the body and head. The idea here is to render a viper harmless by destroying its fangs.

In many discussions of the issue of bridging the gap, a lot of space is spent on the topic of leg movements. Thus, we may see lunging steps, sliding steps, skipping and jumping steps, and hopping or springing forward steps. However, the fact of the matter is that human beings have only two feet, so that in closing a gap, they must either move their front foot first or their back foot first or both simultaneously in springing or jumping forward. Movement is natural, but assessments of timing, tempo, and rhythm are acquired skills. I therefore encourage students to think about combat more abstractly, seeing it not merely as a field of physical movements of arms and legs, but as a social event. Your opponent is a human being with a mind and personality—he is therefore fallible, capable of being deceived and making mistakes. The skilled fighter must be capable of speedily obtaining knowledge of his opponent's strengths and weaknesses and preferred techniques by faking and feinting and must then be able to deceive the opponent so that a fatal mistake is made.

THE THEORY OF KICKING AT THE *CHUM KIL* LEVEL

The *Chum Kil* form introduces three kicks into the Wing Chun system: the ball-of-the-foot lifting kick, the heel kick, and the side-footage kick. This in itself is not a generous supply of kicks. However, further kicks are added at advanced levels of the Wing Chun system, including the *Bil Jee* form (the circling sweep), the wooden-dummy form, and the sticky-leg technique. In addition, I make extensive use of the knee in bridging the gap, charging into an opponent, and smashing my knee against the side of the opponent's knee.

The three kicks found in the *Chum Kil* form have a more or less obvious use. The lifting kick can be used by lifting the ball of your foot into an opponent's groin as he charges into you; in the sticky-leg techniques, this kick can be lifted into an opponent's groin when you have hooked his legs apart with your leg. The heel kick is a well-known frontal attack, and the side-footage kick is an excellent angular attack. Both kicks can theoretically be used as blocks, the idea being to block the opponent's kick at the knee, so that the knee is damaged. The principle here is that the knee or thigh has less angular velocity than the shin or heel, so that an opponent's kick can be jammed with a counter-kick. This all looks good on paper, but against a fast-moving opponent with good footwork, trying to jam his kicks is quite a task. I therefore prefer using deception and fast footwork to fight against a skilled kicker.

There is a lot of confusion among students of Wing Chun

concerning how to defend against kicks, especially the powerful high kicks of *Muay Thai*. Often it is said that hand blocks, such as the *taun sao*, *gum sao*, or *bong sao* may be used. Now, in my opinion, unless you have 32-inch upper arms and 25-inch forearms, this is madness. The angular momentum of a *Muay Thai* round kick, for example, with the full body weight behind it, simply cannot be stopped with your arm by any sort of block. Matters are not improved by attempting to deflect kicks with your arms, an extremely powerful kick may simply sail right through the *taun sao* or *bong sao* blocks, collapsing the hand move. Also, if you defend against kicks with your hands, then necessarily there will be an opening to your head created for your opponent. Therefore, unless it is absolutely necessary, avoid using your hands to defend against kicks. Instead, move out of the way of the kick, either jamming the kick by moving forward, or by moving backward or to the left or right—and counter-attack at the first opening.

Wing Chun kung-fu is typically characterized as a low kicking style, all kicks being directed below the belt. Indeed, China's Futshan Pai style of Wing Chun directs all of its kicks below the knee, restricting kicking to the leg attacks employed in sticky-leg fighting. In general, Wing Chun fighters are very much concerned with balance, and there can be no doubt that high kicks leave a fighter in a position of relative imbalance. If the kick misses, you might have your supporting leg kicked out from under you, or an opponent may charge into you, knocking you down. However, the high kicks do have certain advantages over hand attacks. First, while kicks are generally slower than punches, kicks are generally more powerful than punches, because of the strength of the leg muscles. Second, the leg has a greater reach than the arm, which is an advantage in fighting, all other things being equal. Third, since most people wear shoes on the street, the foot is usually better protected than the hand—this is an obvious advantage in self-defense.

Considering all of these points, we can see that kicking involves what economists call an opportunity cost: certain advantages also have associated with them certain disadvantages. What this means for a philosophy of kicking is that if an opening exists for a high kick to the head, you must accept the fact of momentary relative imbalance and plan an appropriate defense. I therefore see no reason to recommend a ban on high kicking in street fighting, provided that it is done intelligently and fast, exploiting any openings or mistakes made by the opponent. Nevertheless, the speed, flexibility, and versatility of the hand make it an ideal weapon for the Wing Chun fighter, especially when that inevitable aspect of the human condition, aging, reduces the speed and flexibility of your leg.

IMPORTANT HAND MOVES OF THE *CHUM KIL* FORM

I shall not discuss here every hand move of the *Chum Kil* form, because many of these moves have an obvious physical meaning that can be best illustrated by the photographs. Keeping with my desire to expose and scientifically analyze the so-called secret techniques of Wing Chun kung-fu, I shall discuss only the seemingly unusual hand movements that have a subtle meaning.

1. THE PIERCING HAND MOVEMENT
This movement in the opening of the *Chum Kil* form is more than just a double-finger thrust employing an interesting and useful combat principle. In the form, both hands are pushed out from the center-line (median axis of the body), employing a grinding type of push. On the third circle, the hands are raised so that the fingers point down, with the side of the wrists facing up. Then one thrusts down and then up, with a bouncing, ricocheting action. The idea is to bounce a punch or finger strike off of an opponent's guard, or in the former move, to grind an attack straight through the guard.

2. THE DOUBLE-ARM BAR
The double-arm bar in the first section of the *Chum Kil* form is not used as a block: recall that in Wing Chun, we prefer not to use two hands to block or deflect an attack. The double-arm bar is a convenient way of training the coordination of raising the elbow into an arm bar or half *bong sao,* with a pivot from left to right, and from right to left. In this movement there is a subtle gem that is worth describing: this is the slight drop of the elbows in the pivot from one side to the next. The important combat application of this is that a defensive *bong sao* is rather weak from the side, and this is where a Wing Chun fighter aims to attack, pushing on your triceps to lock up your arm and render you trapped and helpless. But by dropping the elbow, the leverage situation is changed and the opponent's hands

are forced down, and an opening is created for your own attack to the opponent's head.

3. THE SINGLE-ARM BAR AND *TAUN SAO*

This movement also occurs in the first section of the *Chum Kil* form. It is used as a close-range defense against a punch, and is performed by placing the *taun sao* over the top of the punch, and then positioning the other hand which forms the bar underneath. The opponent is then held in a position in which you could hit him with either hand. Alternatively, there is an excellent technique that could be used that virtually guarantees a hit, known as the licking hand. Grab the opponent's hand and jerk him forward to disrupt his balance. With your other hand, slap his groin with a palm-open back-hand strike. Now the first hand glides around the side of the opponent's body, delivering a palm strike to the ear. A further palm strike to the face is delivered by the hand that struck the groin. The idea here is to hit your opponent with a fast combination of open-hand strikes while he is off balance. This technique is called the licking hand because your hand licks over the surface of the opponent's body. For more on this concept of fighting, see the next chapter on the *Bil Jee* form.

4. THE CHICKEN-WING *BONG SAO*

This type of *bong sao,* found in the first section of the *Chum Kil* form, is a low *bong sao* formed down the side of the body with the elbow slightly bent and the fingers pointing away from the body to tense the forearm muscles. This hand move has a number of uses, but is primarily used in Wing Chun's *chin-na* (grappling and seizing) techniques, to dislocate the shoulder. If the opponent's arm is caught in a lock, or grabbed by the claw digging into the pressure points on the arm, the opponent's arm may be struck with the chicken-wing *bong sao.* Dislocation occurs because by using footwork and/or body rotation, the entire momentum of the attacker's body is concentrated behind the blow.

5. SIDE-HIGH *BONG SAO* AND SIDE *TAUN SAO*

The sequence of high *bong saos* to the side and side *taun saos* in the second section of the *Chum Kil* form is used to train the student to move fluidly from a *bong sao* to a *taun sao* to protect the side after a head defense. In addition, the drop from a *bong sao* to a *taun sao* is, as I pointed out above, a convenient way of freeing a trapped *bong sao* by altering the leverage situation.

6. DOUBLE LOW FRONT *BONG SAO*

This movement is not used as a block or deflection. Its principal use is to enable one to break out of a bear hug (from the rear over the arms), by taking a step to disrupt your opponent's balance, then thrusting down to free your own hands. The important thing here is not the *bong sao* itself but the principle behind its use. Certain locks can be broken by footwork, by moving to both disrupt the attacker's balance and change the leverage situation. I shall discuss ways of breaking locks in more detail in the third book in this series, *Weapons and Advanced Techniques,* in the chapter dealing with Wing Chun's *chin-na* techniques.

61   62

63

THE *CHUM KIL* FORM

The form opens as in the *Sil Lum Tao*, with the movements depicted in Figures 1–13.

SECTION 1

61. Remain at attention, in the parallel stance (Wing Chun training stance), as described in the *Sil Lum Tao* form. Since the *Chum Kil* form, as well as the *Bil Jee* form, involve footwork, no internal training or *Chi Kung* is performed.

62–64. Place both hands in front of your chest as shown (62), with

64   65   66

67   68   69

both hands in the *wu sao* (defensive hand position), your wrists about a fist-and-a-half's distance from your chest. In a relaxed fashion, push your hands forward in an arc (63), so that when your arms are extended as far as a normal lead defense, they have risen to about face level. Move your hands back to the starting point (64), so that you have traced an ellipse through your center-line. The grinding-hands movement is used to grind over a guard and then strike much like a bulldozer moving over rubble. Perform this movement twice.

65–66. On the third ellipse movement at the position shown (65), with the hands raised high at face level, execute a double *bil jee*,

70   71   72

or finger thrust (66). The thrust involves a slight downward curve, and then an upward arc, as the hands near full extension, like a bullet ricocheting off a hard surface. The attack is used to penetrate a strong defensive guard, by attempting to bounce one's attack over the guard—to deflect the guard slightly on the downward arc and then bounce over the top.

67–68.   From the double *bil jee*, or finger thrust, immediately pivot to the left, forming the double bar arm shown in Figure 37 of the *Sil Lum Tao* form (67). When pivoting to the left, have the left arm on top; and when pivoting to the right, have the right arm on top. Pivot to the left, then to the right, to the left again, and finally to the right, as shown in the photograph (68). This technique trains the coordination of pivoting and the defensive and offensive use of the elbow. The pivot also has an important use, as we shall see in a later volume, in advanced sticky-hands (*chi sao*) techniques.

69.   From the double bar arm, deliver a double *bil jee* at throat level to an imaginary opponent.

70.   Then drop the arms into a double *taun sao*. The dropping movement is an important defense against upper cuts to the solar plexus region.

71–72.   Now perform a right *taun sao* with a forearm slap, which is sometimes called the arm-breaking technique (71). As you slap your forearm, there is an upward jolt added to the motion by your palm. This technique trains Wing Chun students in the use of leverage as well as in the application of what is known as inch-force in

THE *CHUM KIL* FORM AND FOOTWORK • **45**

73   74   75

attacking an opponent's joints. Perform this jolting *taun sao* movement in this sequence: right *taun sao,* left slap (71); left *taun sao,* right slap (72); and, once again, right *taun sao,* left slap.

73.   Deliver a left palm strike (fingers face up), with the right hand held in the rear guard position.

74.   Then deliver a right palm strike (fingers face up), with the left hand held in the rear guard position.

75.   Now deliver a left palm strike (fingers face up), simultaneously pulling your right arm back to the position in which it is held while at attention, as shown in Figure 61 of the *Chum Kil* form.

76.   Pivot 180 degrees to the left. Simultaneously form a single bar arm with your left arm.

77.   Take one step with your left foot, sliding up the right foot. Simultaneously form a right *taun sao* that rests upon the inner forearm of the left single bar arm.

78.   Pivot 90 degrees to the right. Perform a chicken-wing, or lower *bong sao,* with your left arm. The arm is extended by the side about a fist-and-a-half's distance from the body, the blade of the hand facing out like the extended wing of a bird. The right guard hand is held low. This technique, performed with a pivot, is a sweeping deflection used against low punches and kicks. At advanced levels, it can be used in grappling and throwing techniques.

Now pivot around 90 degrees to the position you previously occupied, immediately returning to the single bar arm stance

76   77   78

79   80   81

shown in Figure 76 above. Then repeat exactly the instructions for Figures 76–78 two more times. After returning to
the single bar arm formation for the third time, proceed as
follows.

79.   Now place your right arm, which has formed a fist behind the
single bar arm. Pause for a moment.

80.   Deliver a right punch. Simultaneously withdraw your left arm
to your chest, as shown in Figure 61.

81.   Now pivot immediately 90 degrees to the right. As you do so,
deliver a 180-degree chop with your right hand.

82   83

84

82. Return the chopping arm to the center-line, performing a right *jut sao,* or downward deflection of the heel of the hand. When the *jut sao* has been executed, the right arm is in the *wu sao,* or defensive hand position, described earlier (72–74). Note that this hand is slightly closer to the body than the lead hand usually is in the normal fighting stance. Put your left hand, fingers fully extended, on the crook of your wrist.

83. Now deliver a left *bil jee,* or finger thrust, simultaneously pulling back your right fist to your chest, as it is held in the attention position.

84. Withdraw your left hand and return to the basic attention position.

Now repeat the above sequence of movements (62–84), on the opposite side. When you have finished, return to the basic attention position to complete Section 1 of the *Chum Kil* form.

85

86

SECTION 2

85. Begin Section 2 of the *Chum Kil* form by pivoting 90 degrees to the left and forming a closed-fist single bar arm with the left arm. The right arm is pulled back and the right fist is held close to the chest as shown in Figure 61. The closed-fist bar arm is used more for offense, while the open-handed bar arm is particularly useful for sensitivity in *chi sao,* or sticky-hand, techniques.

86. Deliver a Wing Chun lifting kick with the left foot: with the knee straight and the toes rigid, lift the leg upward, approximately at a right angle to the supporting leg. This kick is used to lift between an opponent's legs, into the groin.

87   88   89

87. Now set your left foot down, and slide up your right foot to maintain your stance. While your feet face in the direction of the kick, twist your body 90 degrees right of the direction of movement and perform a high *bong sao* (a side *bong sao*) with your right arm.

88. Drop your elbow to defend the side of the body, which was exposed when the *bong sao* was used. The right arm forms a low *taun sao,* with the left hand resting upon its wrist. This hand formation is a classical form, not an effective defensive skill. The important skill to be mastered here is the technique of dropping the elbow.

89. Repeat the sequence described in Figures 87 and 88—step, *bong sao,* elbow drop—two more times. In the second sequence, when you reach the side *bong sao* position, turn your body to the front and deliver a right back-fist into your center-line. Then conclude the first half of Section 2 of the *Chum Kil* form by performing a pivot and a chop, *jut sao* and *Bil Jee,* as already seen

90   91   92

in Section 1 of this form (81–84). Return to the basic attention position.

Repeat the above sequence (85–89) on the opposite side to complete Section 2 of the *Chum Kil* form.

SECTION 3

90.   Begin Section 3 of the *Chum Kil* form by pivoting to the left 90 degrees from the basic attention position, hands still held back against your chest.

91.   Deliver a high heel kick with the front foot.

92.   Put the kicking foot down and step forward, sliding up the rear foot. Simultaneously perform a double lower *bong sao*. The arms are bent at about 150 degrees, the blades of the hands facing toward

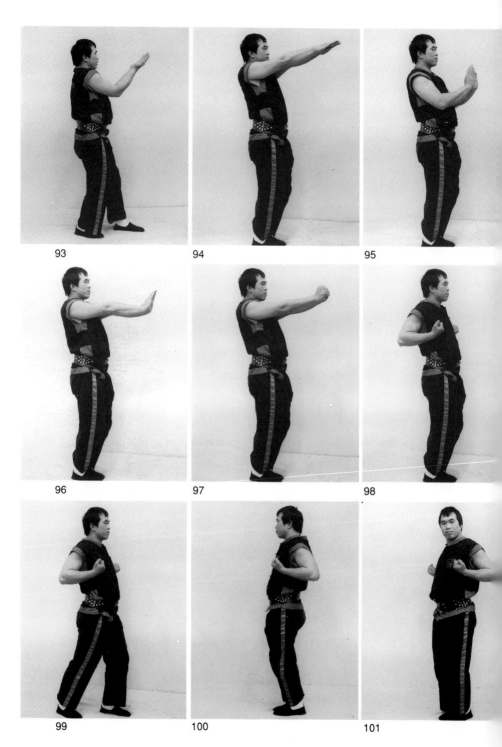

93

94

95

96

97

98

99

100

101

102   103   104

the opponent. This technique is sometimes used as a mid-section block, but in general it is not preferred because it involves using two hands in defense.

93.   Take a step forward and defend your head with a double *taun sao*.

94.   Step in with your back foot and deliver a double *bil jee* to eye level. Your feet remain together.

95.   Drop your hands down into a double *jut sao* to defend your chest.

96.   Then deliver a double palm strike through your center-line.

97.   Form two fists.

98.   Withdraw the fists to the chest.

99.   Step backward and pivot 180 degrees in the opposite direction. Repeat the double *bong sao*/double *taun sao* sequence described above (92, 93), only in the opposite direction.

100.   Having completed the double *bong sao*/double *taun sao* sequence, pull your arms back. You are now in the position shown in Figure 98, only on the opposite side.

101.   Now pivot 45 degrees to the left.

102.   Deliver a side-footage kick, a kick executed at 45 degrees to your center-line. As in karate, it is typically used as a block and as an offensive weapon.

103–4.   Step down and deliver a *gum sao,* or downward depressing palm strike, with your left hand, as shown in Figure 103. Then pivot your feet 180 degrees to the left and deliver another *gum*

THE *CHUM KIL* FORM AND FOOTWORK • **53**

105   106

sao with your right hand (104), and then pivot right 180 degrees, then do one more right *gum sao*. This is primarily a defense against a knee attack. However in both 103 and 104, keep your trunk at a 45-degree angle to the front. Only pivot your trunk 90 degrees when your feet pivot 180 degrees.

105.   Pivot left 90 degrees into the parallel stance and deliver three punches in the sequence: left, right, and left. Withdraw the fists to the chest and shuffle both feet into the basic attention position.

106.   Conclude the *Chum Kil* form in exactly the same way as you concluded the *Sil Lum Tao* form: Move your heels in together, and then your toes. Straighten your legs. This is the reverse of the opening of the form. Standing with your feet together, slowly move your hands down by your sides in depressing side palm strikes, while exhaling.

This concludes the *Chum Kil* form.

3

The *Bil Jee* Form

INTRODUCTION

Wing Chun's *Bil Jee* form, or the thrusting-fingers form, was traditionally taught only to the most trusted students; it was said not to go out of the door. But such legendary social secrecy—and indeed all talk of transmission of secret teachings or of any secret techniques—has no place whatsoever in any rational and analytical approach to an understanding of the knowledge to be found within the many differing systems of the martial arts.

As I have done in previous chapters with the forms known as *Sil Lum Tao* and *Chum Kil,* I shall now explain the physical meaning and significance of the *Bil Jee* form. Unlike the two previous forms, the *Bil Jee* form—which features finger strikes, the most useful striking movement in Wing Chun—does not consist of three parts comprising a sequence of different hand movements; rather, it is made up of a number of parts each having some central theme that is repeated and emphasized a number of times.

PRINCIPAL ATTACKING WEAPONS

The principle attacking weapons of the *Bil Jee* form are the elbow, palm, and fingertips. These strikes are only fully explicable by an explanation of their use in sticky-hand fighting, and I shall have much more to say about this in the second book in this series, *Fighting and Grappling.*

First, let us look at the elbow movement. The elbow in Wing Chun can be used as it is used in *Muay Thai:* as a primary close-range striking weapon. As such, because of the sharpness of the elbow bone, it is a devastating weapon—it is often called the king of the arm. The elbow in the *Bil Jee* form can be used as a high-to-low smash, but it can also be used to knock down a guard.

For example, you may defend against a straight punch by countering with a *bong sao,* and then in one fluid movement drag the opponent's arm down with your descending elbow, and whip a back-fist into his face, as the back-fist technique fits in very naturally with the *Bil Jee* elbow.

The palm strikes and finger strikes in the *Bil Jee* form are concerned with close-body, under-the-bridge attacks. By an under-the-bridge attack, I mean aggressive action that enters under the opponent's guard. Finger strikes are used to glide across the body, under the guard to attack the throat.

Consequently, the most important finger strike is the *bil jee,* or palm-down strike, because this is the natural hand shape for touching (also, the palm-up finger strike can jar and injure the fingers). These finger strikes are often made by attacking from only inches away from the throat, using a jarring movement employing what is known as inch-force, since it usually takes place entirely within the space of an inch or two. Such an attack, when performed adeptly with both speed and power, is virtually impossible to defend against if the hands are trapped because of a sticky-hand technique.

AN ANALYSIS OF SELECTED *BIL JEE* TECHNIQUES

Circling Foot Sweep. The circling foot sweep found in the early part of the *Bil Jee* form is an elementary part of sticky-leg fighting. The circle in question is formed by the motion of a foot as it moves from having first locked up the front of an opponent's leg to sweeping the leg off the ground—by striking the back of the opponent's lower leg with the back of your lower leg. In this sweep, the toes remain in contact with the ground at all times for the sake of balance, and only the heel is lifted. As the opponent's leg is swept, he can be pushed over backward.

Grappling Hand and Palm Strikes. These movements symbolize another subtle Wing Chun fighting principle: pulling an opponent into a strike to maximize its force. In the *Sil Lum Tao* form, students are taught the grab-and-punch technique. This involves defending against a punch with *bong sao, tan sao,* or *til sao* techniques, which slow the punch down so that it can be grabbed; once the hand is seized, the opponent is pulled into a punch. This is an excellent way of maximizing punching power because of the momentum given to the opponent's body by the grab and pull. It is also an effective way to disrupt an opponent's timing by momentarily disrupting his balance.

In the *Bil Jee* form, the student learns a more complicated form of this technique. The *bong sao, taun sao,* or virtually any other defensive hand formation, may be suddenly pulled, to clear an opening for a strike. A good example of this is to pull the hand of an opponent's *bong sao,* so that the elbow drops and your punch sails over the flattened *bong sao* . The physical actions of pushing and pulling have not been systematized into comprehensive fighting skills in much of Chinese kung-fu; the effectiveness of these activities in many forms of wrestling (especially Sumo) testifies to its merits.

Overhead Heel-of-the-Palm Strike and Hammer Punch. These two parts of the body are very much neglected as attacking weapons, but they may well be the most devastating hand attacks available to Wing Chun students. The overhead palm strike is delivered so that impact is made with the cushioned bone along the edge of the heel of the palm, while the hammer punch is made with the fleshy lower edge of the fist. Both of these areas are capable of withstanding considerable punishment without sustaining any substantial injury, making them ideal attacking weapons. Furthermore, considerable momentum can be gathered from an overhead strike due to the combined effect of gravity and the involvement of the muscles of the shoulder, back, and triceps. In sticky-hand fighting, either of these techniques can be executed from the *bong sao* hand. From the *bong sao* technique, rotate your hand inward, toward your center-line, then cut down upon your opponent's head.

Side-Asking Hand and Tracing-the-Shape Palm.   The side-asking hand is a method of deflection that is related to the *til sao* technique from the *Sil Lum Tao* form. Both of these hand movements are security defenses, designed to cover a wide area of the upper body by an upward arm movement. The *til sao* is used to cover the front of the body, while the side-asking hand covers the side. In some forms of Wing Chun, the *Bil Jee* form employs the tracing-the-shape palm movement (so called because the hands stick to and follow the opponent's) instead of the side-asking hand. In the form, this movement consists of a double push to the side; this move in itself seems somewhat unimpressive. However, in actual combat, this move is invaluable in sticky-hand in-fighting. The idea is to cling to your opponent's elbows with your palms, with the ultimate aim of pinning one or more of his elbows to his body. If this can be done, then the opponent is, for all effective purposes, momentarily trapped, and a clear opening for a strike to the head will exist.

Above, I mentioned the importance of the physical activities of pushing and pulling to sticky-hand fighting, and at this point I would like to re-emphasize the importance of these techniques. Not only may one get through an opponent's guard by pulling the defensive hands, but openings can also be created by pushing the defensive hands, either up, down, or to the left or the right. Not only does this create an opening; it can also leave the opponent helpless for an instant: an arm that has been pushed up in the air above the opponent's own head is effectively dead until the opponent can run away using defensive footwork. That split second, though, is all it takes for a good fighter to do damage.

The Tor *Hand.*   While on the topic of opening up and destroying an opponent's guard, it is worthwhile briefly mentioning the *tor* hand movement. This movement occurs in the *Bil Jee* form after the side-asking hand or the tracing-the-shape palm. The *tor* is really a modified *fook sao* with the fingers facing downward. It is part of a sequence that is taught at the *Sil Lum Tao* level, where an opponent's guard is hooked by the *fook sao,* and then by the *haun sao,* or wrist-twisting technique, the guard is opened up and a palm strike is delivered to an open target, such as the floating ribs. At one point in this sequence, the hand is in the *tor* shape. At the *Bil Jee* level, students are taught to add a pivot of the feet to this sequence to disrupt the opponent's balance as well as to add power to the strike.

The Closing of Bil Jee.   The closing of the *Bil Jee* form consists of the practitioner bending over in such a way that the fingertips of both hands (held together touching at the palms, fingers straight), touch the ground. Then the practitioner rises and rotates his arms, flinging them around in circles. There is a lot of useless debate in Wing Chun circles about the hidden meaning of this. Some say that it is a Buddhist prayer, some sort of physical meditation like the worshiping of the Buddha by the *wu sao* hand-form in the *Sil Lum Tao* . Others say that in this sequence you are bending over to pick up sand to fling at your opponent, while others yet again see it only as a type of exercise.

Whatever the reader's opinion, it is worth keeping in mind that there is a danger in over-literally interpreting the movements within the forms, so that absolutely every movement has profound combat significance. Chinese kung-fu is a very rich cultural system, and we must not be surprised to find within it symbolic elements that are alien to the Western analytic mentality. Here, I can only hint at some of these religious and symbolic elements and their meaning, and must leave a detailed discussion for another time.

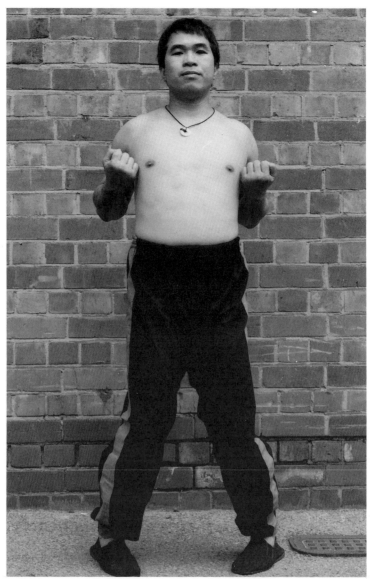

107

THE *BIL JEE* FORM

107.   The *Bil Jee* form begins just like the *Sil Lum Tao* and *Chum Kil* forms, except for the cross-hand movement described below. Start, then, from the parallel stance in the attention position.

108.   Deliver a straight left punch through your center-line.

108   109   110

111   112

109.   With your left hand fully extended, flex your wrist, first with fingers pointing up.

110.   Then with fingers pointing down.

111.   Turn your hand over, palm up.

112.   Turn your hand over, palm down.

THE *BIL JEE* FORM • **61**

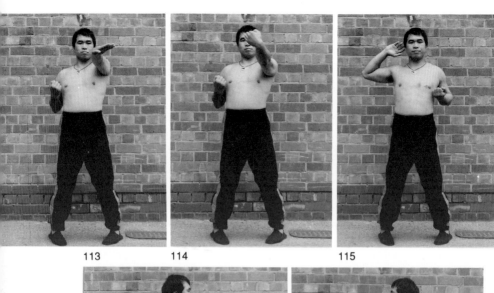

113   114   115

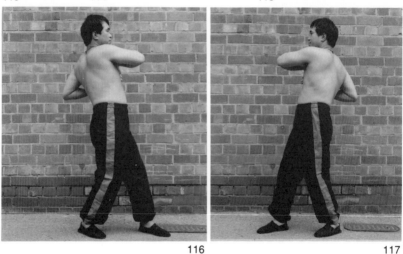

116   117

113.   Turn your hand to the left, palm down.

114.   Perform a *haun sao* rotation of the wrist and withdraw your fist to the attention position.

115.   Place your right open hand by your ear and prepare to pivot and deliver a *Bil Jee* elbow smash.

116.   Pivot 90 degrees to the left and deliver the *Bil Jee* elbow smash. The elbow moves from the position shown in Figure 115 past your ear and down into the center-line. It is an overarm move.

117.   Pivot to the opposite side and deliver a second elbow smash. Then pivot back again and deliver a third and final elbow smash.

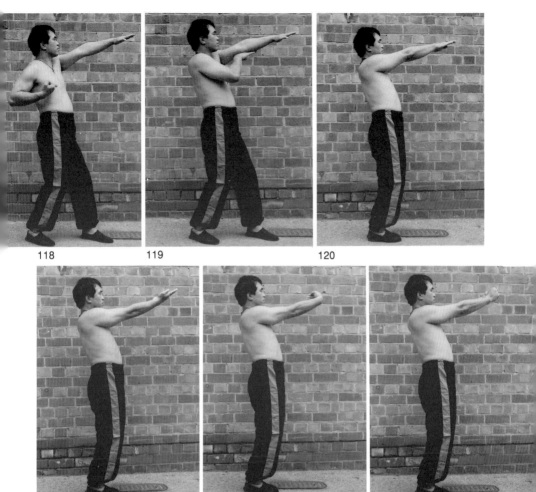

118 119 120

121 122 123

118. Now deliver a *bil jee* strike with your left hand, simultaneously withdrawing your right hand back to form a clenched fist by your chest.

119. Prepare your right hand to make a second *bil jee* strike.

120. Deliver a second *bil jee* strike, with the right hand. Notice the step forward with the back foot to add power to the strike.

121. Now, with hands still fully extended, turn your hands over, palms facing upward.

122. Perform a *haun sao* wrist rotation for 360 degrees; left hand clockwise, right hand counter-clockwise.

123. Form two fists.

124

125

126

127

128

129

124.   Withdraw the fists to your chest, making sure to keep your feet held together.

125.   Begin now to turn 90 degrees to the right (clockwise). In so doing, start to deliver a foot-sweep (as described below) with your right foot.

126.   The sweeping technique, which is shown here, essentially consists of a clockwise, circular movement of the foot, with the heel raised up and the toes kept on the ground. It is used primarily in throwing techniques. Bring the leg back after the foot sweep.

127.   Begin a counter-clockwise foot-sweep with the left foot.

128.   The foot-sweep is half completed.

129.   Complete the foot-sweep and return to the parallel stance at attention.

Now repeat the above sequence of movements (107–29) on the opposite side.

When this has been done, go through the entire sequence of movements two more times, once on the left and once on the right, but while doing the repetitions be sure to perform only *one* elbow smash on the left-hand and the right-hand sides, respectively.

Note that sometimes the form is performed by repeating *all* of the above movements depicted in Figures 107–29 yet again exactly as they are described above!

Note also that there is a high degree of repetition in the *Bil Jee* form; this is in order to reinforce the importance of:

1) the pivot and elbow smash;
2) the *bil jee* strikes; and
3) the foot-sweep.

(Form continued on page 67)

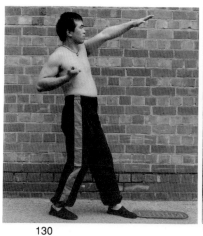
130

131

132

133

134

135

130.   Now having completed the above, from the parallel stance, pivot 90 degrees to the left and deliver a left *bil jee* strike.

131.   Withdraw your left hand to your chest and simultaneously deliver a right side palm strike to face level.

132.   Pivot back to the front and, with the right arm sweeping upward from a low to a high position, perform a side *taun sao,* or asking hand. The arm should be swung in a wide semi-circle from low to high as a defensive maneuver against straight attacks to your side.

133.   Perform a *jut sao* with the right hand. When completed, the left hand should sit upon the crook of the wrist, poised for a *bil jee* strike.

134.   Deliver a left *bil jee* strike and withdraw your right fist to your chest. Then withdraw your left hand and return to the attention posture.

Now repeat all the movements described above (130–34), this time on the opposite side. You should conclude the movements in the basic attention position, facing forward.

135.   Pivot 90 degrees to the left, perform a right elbow smash and then a left *bil jee* strike, followed by a right *bil jee* strike (117–20). Do not pull back the right arm, but retract slightly and snap the wrist into a palm strike.

When you have done that, complete the following sequence of movements, which you have already performed once (132–34) on the opposite side: a side *taun sao,* or asking hand, with the left arm; a *jut sao* with the left hand; and a *bil jee* strike with the right hand. Now withdraw both fists to your chest and stand in the basic attention position.

When you have completed all the movements outlined above, then repeat all of the movements described above in Figure 135—which of course means repeating all of the movements in Figures 132–34 once more as well—on the opposite side.

136   137

138   139   140

136.   Perform a side *taun sao* with your left arm, your right hand forming a *wu sao,* an inner guard hand.

137.   Now deliver a side *taun sao* with your right arm, withdrawing your left fist to your chest.

138.   Perform another side *taun sao,* this time, with your left arm.

139.   Execute a left *jut sao* in your center-line, your right fist held by your chest.

140.   Pivot 90 degrees to the left and perform a *tor sao* with the left hand. A *tor sao* is a *fook sao* (hooking hand move) with a pivot. It is used for moving away a guarding arm so that a strike can be landed.

141

142

Perform the *tor sao,* first to the right, and then again to the
left. Conclude with the familiar *jut sao/bil jee* sequence
(133–34). Face front in the basic attention position.

Now repeat the movements described in Figures 136–39
on the opposite side. Face front in the attention position.

141.   Pivot 90 degrees to the left. Perform a *taun sao* with the
right hand and a *gaun sao* (downward deflecting chop) with the left.
142.   Pivot to the opposite side 180 degrees, performing a left
taun sao and a right *gaun sao.*

Now repeat the movements described above (141–42).
Conclude once more with the *jut sao/bil jee* sequence
(133–34). Then repeat these movements on the opposite
side. Face the front in the attention position.

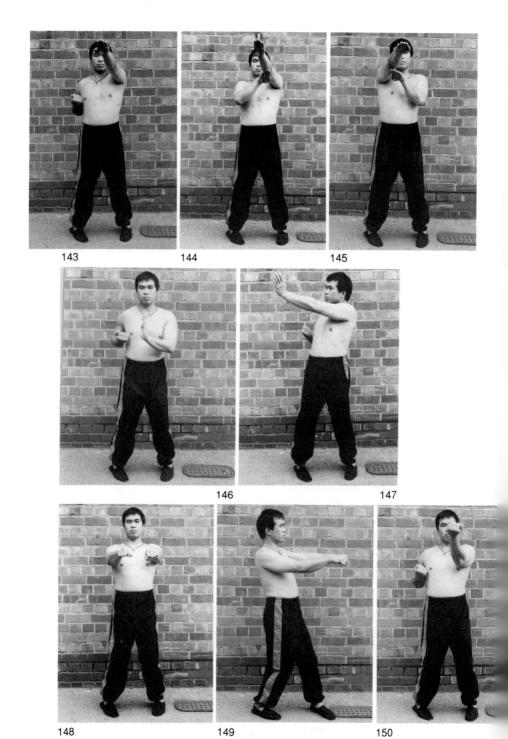

143   144   145

146   147

148   149   150

143.   Deliver a left *bil jee.*

144.   Throw a follow-up right *bil jee* with the left arm still fully extended.

145.   Throw a left *bil jee* with the right arm still fully extended.

146.   Withdraw your right fist to your chest. Bring your left hand to the *wu sao* position in your center-line, about a fist-and-a-half's width from your chest.

147.   Strike with your left hand, cutting across your body to your right, and perform a cross-body, cutting-edge palm strike at the opponent's head.

Conclude then with the *jut sao/ bil jee* sequence again. Face the front in the attention position.

Now repeat all of these movements, which are described above in Figures 143–47, once again but on the opposite side, and also the *jut sao/bil jee* sequence (133–34).

When you have completed the repetition, then face the front in the attention position.

148.   Place both fists in the center-line.

149.   Pivot to the left 90 degrees.

150.   Pivot back to the front and deliver a left back fist, or hammer punch.

Conclude with the *jut sao/ bil jee* sequence. Face the front in the attention position.

Now repeat all of these movements, which are described above in Figures 148–50, including the *jut sao/bil jee* sequence once again, but on the opposite side.

When you have completed the repetition, then face the front in the attention position.

(Form continued on page 72)

151 152 153

154 155 156

151–54. With the hands in the center-line, held in prayer-like fashion (151), drop both hands down (152), swing back and up around the side of the body twice, and then reverse the direction (153). Bend down (154), touching the ground with the tips of your fingers. These movements are a classical exercise, although some view the overhead chopping movement (153) as a double axe handed attack. The movements, therefore, constitute a controversial aspect of the *Bil Jee* form.

155. Deliver three punches—left, right, and left.

156. Conclude the *Bil Jee* form in exactly the same way as you concluded the *Sil Lum Tao* and *Chum Kil* forms: Move your heels in together, and then your toes. Straighten your legs. This is the reverse of the opening of the form. Standing with your feet together, slowly move your hands down by your sides in depressing side palm strikes, while exhaling.

This concludes the *Bil Jee* form.

157

COMBAT APPLICATIONS OF THE *BIL JEE* FORM

It is not my aim here to give any exhaustively comprehensive outline of combat applications of the forms, that task is reserved for later volumes. For this introductory volume, which has performed the needed task of presenting the scientific foundation of Wing Chun kung-fu, I will illustrate some basic street-fighting techniques, as a taste of what is to be presented in later volumes.

157.   The Wing Chun fighter (right), in the system's fighting stance, squares off against a larger opponent in an open, bare-knuckle boxing stance. Notice the weakness of the hand formation: first, the over-extended left arm, which leaves the head exposed, and the right arm, which is held too close to the body, and is thus ineffectual as a defensive block. In the sequence of techniques to follow, let this position be known as the starting position.

158

159

160

161

158. The Wing Chun fighter exploits the weakness in his opponent's guard. Stepping forward, moving the right foot one step, and also sliding the left foot one step to maintain the stance, the Wing Chun student sticks to the larger man's over-extended left arm. This is a clear application of Wing Chun's *chi sao* technique. In essence, one maintains contact with the opponent's arm, neutralizing any other attacks by deflection, as a trained *chi sao* proponent can feel an oncoming attack via muscular movement in the opponent's arm.

159. Having penetrated the opponent's guard, a side-palm attack is made through the center-line to the larger opponent's neck. Notice that the larger opponent's right arm is pressed against his chest, constituting an elementary Wing Chun arm trap. The larger opponent is now completely open, and hence strategically vulnerable, and multiple attacks can be delivered in quick succession.

160. From the starting position (*see* Figure 157), the larger opponent delivers a left straight-arm punch, which is deflected by a *taun sao*. A step has been taken to close the range, or bridge the gap.

161. The larger opponent's left arm is grabbed by the left hand

THE *BIL JEE* FORM • **75**

162   163   164

of the Wing Chun fighter, while a right straight-arm punch is returned. An attempt is made by the larger man to stop this punch. However, as his inner guard hand was held far too close to his face, he is incapable of stopping the punch, which breaks through the guard into his face.

162.   The larger man is now open on the right, and at this range, a *Bil Jee* elbow strike fits successfully through this opening.

163.   Return to the combat situation depicted in Figure 160, where the larger opponent has launched a left straight-arm punch, which has been countered by the Wing Chun proponent with a *taun sao,* a forwardly thrusted deflecting defense. Contact is maintained with the opponent's arm (by sticky-hands). A grappling hand move is applied, simultaneously with a left kick to the knee. This generates extra force with which to snap the opponent's body forward in a whiplash fashion, breaking the knee.

164.   This attack is immediately followed up with a powerful punch to the upper jaw, with a second kick to the knee—this time from the right—involving a stomping down action on the back of the opponent's injured knee.

165   166   167

165.   Alternatively from the situation depicted in Figure 163, the larger opponent's left arm may be restrained by a bar arm lock. (A bar arm is simply a grappling move that applies force or leverage to the elbow joint in a direction against its natural path of movement.) From this, a hammer punch or forearm blow to the elbow joint could be delivered. The larger man's weak stance and his poor stability mean that he can easily be set off balance.

166.   It is now easy—having controlled and neutralized the opponent's left lead arm, and having got in on the opponent's side, so that his own body cuts off effective defense by his right arm—to attack the throat with the Wing Chun claw-hand. Notice that control is maintained over the larger man's left arm throughout the attack.

167.   The opponent's throat can also be attacked under the bridge, that is, from under the lead attacking arm. Here we can see how the larger man's left arm is locked in a bar arm across the Wing Chun fighter's chest. Notice how the Wing Chun fighter sticks to the opponent's leg: a slight sweep of the larger man's left foot would cause him to fall backward, making him break his own elbow. Figure 167 illustrates the difference between Wing Chun throws and those

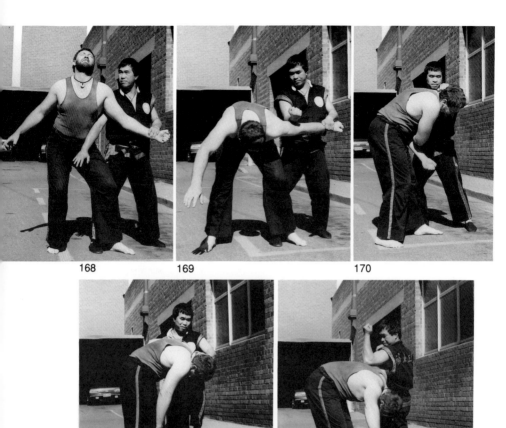

168   169   170

171   172

from other arts: these techniques are for self-defense and must be used with caution, only in life-or-death situations.

168.   The groin can now be readily attacked with either a slap, chop, or claw-hand.

169.   As the opponent bends forward in pain, a forearm smash to the elbow joint is delivered.

170.   The opponent grasps his own injured left arm, while the Wing Chun fighter grabs him by the hair.

171.   The larger man's head is pulled down onto a knee strike.

172.   Then an elbow smash is delivered to the opponent's back, neutralizing him.

173

174

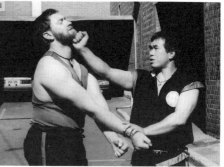

175

176

173.   Consider another attack, this time a short-range (left) Wing Chun punch, a hammer punch. We can see here how this·attack is stopped with a *bong sao* . Notice the excellent head defense of the Wing Chun fighter, and observe how easy it is to grab the larger man's left arm.

174.   The left arm is now grabbed and jerked down, and a back fist is delivered to the jaw. However, although stunned, the larger opponent retaliates with a close-range Wing Chun punch from the right.

175.   The Wing Chun fighter deflects the attack with a right *taun sao*.

176.   At this point a Wing Chun hand trap is applied. This is only a simple technique, and a later volume shall explain the theory of this in detail. The fighter's top arm cuts down the opponent's lower arm, so that the opponent's arms are crossed or tied up. Then the defender's hands are switched so that his left is used to check the opponent's arms. This gives the Wing Chun fighter an opportunity to deliver a straight punch to the jaw, since the opponent is rendered incapable of defending himself.

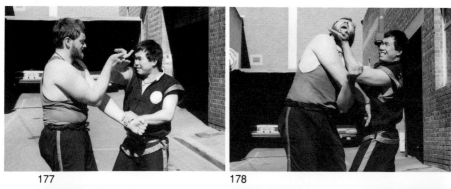

177   178

                        179   180

177. In any martial-arts practice, things may not always go as planned, and a knowledgeable adversary may counter your favorite techniques. This has occurred here, where the Wing Chun fighter's punch has been stopped by the larger man's *taun sao*. The larger man's left arm, however, has been re-grabbed. Notice the Wing Chun fighter's fingers set to grab the opponent's right arm.

178. The *taun sao* of the larger opponent is then cut down, so that his right arm is crossed over his left arm. The Wing Chun proponent then strikes with a palm-strike to the chin. Note that the left elbow of the Wing Chun fighter effectively locks over the top of both arms of the larger fighter, virtually tying his arms in a knot.

179.   A less complex counterattack to the situation depicted in Figure 177 would be to simply grab the opponent's right *taun sao* and jerk the arm down suddenly, while simultaneously chopping with your left arm.

180.   Suppose that the previous technique is executed, but that the larger proponent stops the chop with a *taun sao*. The *taun sao*

181

182

183

used by the larger man is incorrect, and hence it is a weak defense, because the angle between his biceps and forearm is less than 90 degrees. A counter-punch could break through this defense.

181. Instead of punching, a more complex counterattack is delivered. The larger man's left arm is twisted upon his right, and, in the process, the left arm is straightened. Both arms are effectively locked by the force applied to the larger man's right arm. At this point, it is possible to break the larger man's left arm at the elbow.

182–83. The Wing Chun man now delivers a punching attack. A hand trap is maintained by holding the larger man's arms with the right hand, while punching with the left (182), and then holding with the left, while punching with the right (183). This chain-punching can be repeated as long as the hand trap is maintained, by pressing the larger opponent's arms onto his body.

Illustration of techniques such as these will be given in more detail in volumes two and three, now that knowledge of the scientific foundations of the martial art of Wing Chun has been explained in this volume.

4

Conditioning, Stretching, and Power Training

INTRODUCTION

No study of a martial art is complete without a discussion of training methods. In this chapter, I shall discuss the following methods: 1) iron-palm training; 2) weight training; 3) flexibility training; 4) speed training; and 5) aerobic and anaerobic fitness; presenting a logical and scientific method of training for the student of Wing Chun kung-fu.

1. IRON-PALM TRAINING

Kung-fu is a Chinese term that may be defined as an intense concentration of effort. *Kung* is similar to the intense energy that an angry cat has, and it is *kung* that enables desperate parents to lift cars off their children in traffic accidents. In cases such as these, the use of *kung* is involuntary. The student of the martial arts attempts to control this force and make its use voluntary.

The Chinese recognize two basic types of *kung:* internal and external. The internal system, *yin* or negative *kung,* makes use of the control of *chi* and meditation to build terrifying powers. In this book I do not deal extensively with the topic of negative *kung,* as I am skeptical about its existence. It is sufficient though to list some results of negative *kung* that the Chinese believe can be obtained by years of intense training.

Two hard-to-believe examples of negative *kung* are red-sand palm *kung* and finger *kung,* which are allegedly forms of distance killing where it is believed that one can injure or even kill an assailant from a distance without physically touching the body. Other forms of negative *kung* are not as spectacular and should be viewed with less scepticism by the Western mind. To strengthen the palm and finger tips, *chi* must emanate from the *tan-t'ien*—the traditional store-house of *chi* located about three inches below the navel—to the palm and fingertips. For the Chinese, the *tan-t'ien* represents the focus where we can achieve a unity of the physical and mental forces of the body, combining respiration (breath), mental concentration, and the physical energy of the muscles of the body. *Chi Kung* training, as I have mentioned elsewhere in this book, is a vast subject that is not easily summarized. It is sufficient to point out that there are various sets of *Chi Kung* breathing and visualization exercises, both of which train a martial artist to direct *chi* to a certain part of the body at will. The attacking weapons of the body are thought to be gradually strengthened by this concentrated flow of *chi* without disfigurement of the limbs and feet by callouses, and the body is also conditioned to receive blows without substantial injuries. The *Chi Kung* practitioner is often said to have a cotton stomach, to wear a shirt of iron, and to have iron limbs.

External *kung, yang* or positive *kung,* is the more widely practiced form of *kung* training and the one in which results are quickly achieved by the dedicated. Although the use of the concentration of *chi* also features in this method of training, the focus of this training is upon the development of the strength of skeletal muscles, tendons, and ligaments, as well as on the conditioning of the striking weapons of the body by the formation of protective callouses. But external *kung* in Wing Chun has its soft aspect: the striking weapons of the body are soaked in an herbal medicine called *Dit dat jow* (warm-strike-wine) to prevent arthritis, heal bruises, toughen the skin, and relieve pain.

• *BIL JEE* AND EAGLE-CLAW *KUNG*
To train the fingers for striking and clawing, it is necessary to condition the fingertips to withstand blows as well as to increase joint strength.

• EXERCISES TO STRENGTHEN THE FINGERS.
Various gripping exercises can be performed such as squeezing
rubber balls and other grip-strengthening devices. I have found that
there are limits to all of the standard methods, because after a while
you get too strong for the exercise and it becomes too difficult to
overload the finger muscles. I therefore recommend the following
exercises to provide progressive resistance:

   1) *Finger extension.* Use your opposite hand to resist the
extension of your fingers (analogous to leg extension).

   2) *Finger curls (analogous to arm curls).* Again, use your opposite
hand to resist the curling of your fingers. It is also possible to use
dumbbells for this exercise. Bend your fingers at the second knuckle
and use the hook thus formed to lift the weight. Then curl your
fingers into the palm to form a fist. This exercise, neglected by
mainstream body builders, is an excellent forearm developer.

   3)   Wrestle with your fingers, left-hand side versus right-hand
side. Gently stretch the finger muscles.

   4)   Pinch-grip weights. Lift weights by pinching the edge of the
weight with the fingers.

   5)   To develop tearing ability, practice tearing newspapers, tree
bark, and meat from the butchers. Progressive resistance is possible
by merely adding further material to the mass to be torn.

   6)   Obtain a large jar with a wide rim, such that when you lift the
jar by the rim, your fingers are evenly spaced around the rim.
Progressive resistance is possible by filling the jar to various levels
with increasingly heavier materials. It is also possible to do this
exercise by lifting dumbbells end-on with spread fingers.

• CONDITIONING THE HANDS
Callouses are developed by friction and pressure exerted against the
skin. Just as in the development of strength, progressive resistance is
required for increased conditioning. There are two basic methods
for conditioning the striking surfaces of the hand. The first is the
pressure method used in fingertip and knuckle push-ups, or in
pressing your fingertips together with all your strength. The second
is the friction method best experienced after a hard day's gardening.
The idea here is to sandpaper the striking surfaces of the hand,
making the skin tougher. Striking various surfaces combines both

the pressure and friction methods and is the preferred way of conditioning in Wing Chun kung-fu. Begin by striking a bag of flour, and gradually work your way up to striking bags containing harder material such as dried peas, sand, and gun slugs. At all times, use *Dit dat jow,* preferably heated.

• TRAINING THE FOREARM (BRIDGE-HAND)

To increase the strength of the forearm one must overload the forearm muscles with dumbbell exercises involving supination, pronation, flexion, extension, adduction, and circumduction of the wrist. In other words, move your hand in all possible directions against resistance and progressively increase this resistance to overload the forearm muscles.

The best way of conditioning the forearm against blows is to practice the controlled hard blocking of blows with a partner. For example, one may clash a left low *bong sao* against a partner's low *bong sao,* followed by a *taun sao* and a *gaun sao,* then swapping sides. In addition, while hand techniques on the Wing Chun wooden-dummy require soft force, it is also possible to use a strong dummy to condition the forearms and even the palms and knuckles while practicing basic Wing Chun skills. This was apparently a method of training favored by the late Bruce Lee.

• CONDITIONING THE BODY AGAINST BLOWS

The Wing Chun fighter must have a strong trunk built up by various weight exercises for the back and abdominal region. But conditioning against pain is also needed, and there is a way of doing this that is used by the champion kick-boxer Benny "The Jet." At advanced levels, have a partner begin by slapping your abdominal region and gradually work up to taking light and controlled punches. Caution is obviously needed for any trunk conditioning exercise of this sort, but fewer injuries result from this method than from other methods, such as throwing heavy medicine balls. The idea of this training is to experience the pain of combat without incurring an injury, because the amount of force delivered by a responsible training partner can be controlled. It is worth pointing out that various nerve centres of the body—such as the solar plexus—cannot be conditioned and are best defended by developing impenetrable defensive skills.

- CONDITIONING THE FEET

The best way of conditioning the feet is to train in bare feet and spend a lot of time running barefoot over abrasive but safe surfaces. Before you know it, the bottoms of your feet will be like leather. Thai boxers condition their feet for their devastating shin kicks by kicking increasingly hard bags, beginning with bags filled with sand and moving up to gun slugs and beyond. How far the reader goes is a question of how much pain he wishes to endure. The methods are simple; it is the training that is difficult.

It is also possible by means of isometric tension to develop protective muscle on the instep. Lift your toes against the resistance of your hand. Then grip the floor with your toes and contract the foot muscles. In addition, practice standing on the edge of a step supporting your body by your toes, which grip the step like a bird perching. This is excellent training for the sticky-leg skill.

2. WEIGHT AND POWER TRAINING

There are many myths and confusions about weight training, and even more myths about the dangers of weight training for the martial artist—especially that weight training makes one inflexible. For a discussion of these myths, see: T. Anastasio, "Weight Training for the Martial Artist," *Black Belt* **17** (11): 28–31 (November 1979); and Anonymous, "Strength Training for the Martial Artist," *Black Belt* **18** (8): 50–52 (August 1980). In what follows, I state some of the fundamental principles of weight/strength and power training and debunk some of the myths. The reader interested in further information should consult: E. Darden, *The Nautilus Body Building Book* (Chicago: Contemporary Books, 1982); E. Darden, *The Nautilus Advanced Body Building Book* (New York: Simon and Schuster, 1984); J.A. Peterson, ed., *Total Fitness the Nautilus Way* (New York: Leisure Press, 1978); and E. Darden, "Strength Training Principles," *Strength Athlete,* nos. 238–40 (1987). More traditional weight training materials include: E.L. Fox, *Sports Physiology* (Philadelphia: W.B. Saunders, 1979); G.A. Brooks and T.D. Fahey, *Exercise Physiology* (New York: John Wiley and Sons, 1984); D.M. Needham, *Machina Carnis: The Biochemistry of Muscular Contraction in its Historical Development*

(Cambridge: Cambridge University Press, 1971); and J. Atha, "Strengthening Muscle," *Exercise and Sports Sciences Reviews* **9**:1–73 (1981). These books and articles are good because they are concerned with weight training principles along with descriptions of exercises. My major concern is with basic principles and truths, rather than with repeating material found in more detail elsewhere.

• Muscular strength is the amount of force a muscle group can exert against a resistance in one maximal effort.

Power = strength (Force) x velocity.

It follows then that since all martial-arts enthusiasts wish to develop maximum power, they cannot neglect training for muscular strength, together, of course, with speed training.

• Strength training enhances rather than retards one's speed, all other things being equal. Muscles are engines and the fastest car is usually the one capable of generating the most mechanical force. Nor does weight training reduce flexibility, provided stretching is done and full-range motion weight exercises are performed. See Dr. T. Todd, "The Myth of the Muscle-Bound Lifter," *Strength Athlete,* no. 239, 23–25 (April–May 1987).

• To develop muscular strength, a muscle group must be overloaded by being matched against near maximal resistance. Stress must be created so that the muscle physiologically adapts by over-compensation. Progressive resistance must be applied to constantly overload a muscle in order to produce strength gains.

• Muscular endurance is the ability of a muscle group to lift a load over an extended period of time. It has been said that strength training involves low repetitions with high resistance, while muscular endurance requires a light load with high repetitions. However, endurance has also been increased by the former style of strength training.

• Motor skill specificity means that strength development is specific both to the muscle groups exercised and also the pattern of movement. Strength development is also specific to the joint angles at which the muscles are exercised; hence, the need in general for training for strength over the full range of motion of a body part.

• Most people who practice the martial arts are afraid of bulky muscles. However, increasing the strength of a muscle necessarily means increasing size—the cross-sectional diameter of a muscle perpendicular to the direction of the fibers. Muscular hypertrophy itself is due to the increased size of muscle fibers, along with fiber-splitting (hyperplasia), although there is still considerable debate about whether or not fiber-splitting occurs in man. Strength also depends on other mechanical factors such as the size of the body parts serving as simple levers, advantages in leverage provided by the nature of tendon attachments, and neuromuscular efficiency involving the more efficient synchronization of the firing patterns of more muscle fibers. These factors explain why a smaller man may be stronger than a bigger man; they do not prove that muscular strength has nothing to do with muscular size. The martial-arts practitioner's fear of muscular bulk is therefore a fear of strength.

Whether you train using barbells or Nautilus equipment, there are some fundamental principles of weight training which you must adhere to in order to obtain good results.

1. Strength training must involve progressive resistance. You must try to lift increasingly heavy weights with good form. Good form means doing a full range of motion exercises (this being related to the specific excessive muscle group) without cheating by throwing barbells by using other muscles to not merely get the weight in motion but to swing it through virtually the entire range of motion. (The exception to this is negative training, but the down phase of the negative, or the eccentric contraction, must itself be strict). Related to this, see F.A. Hellebrandt and S.J. Houtz, "Mechanisms of Muscle Training in Man: Experimental Demonstration of the Overload Principle," *The Physical Therapy Review* **36** (6): 371–83 (1956).

2. Train until you cannot complete another full performance of the motion, using the maximum available muscle fibers: the higher the intensity, the better stimulated the muscles, provided good and safe form is used. In lifting a weight, make use of compensatory acceleration to give 100% overload of the muscles: push hard every inch of the way rather than at the sticking point. Exerting maximum effort against the weight through the entire range of motion means maximum overload throughout the training session. Therefore, train explosively by maximal pushing, but do not throw weights to fool yourself about your strength level. See J. Toomey, "Explosive Speed: The Key to Tournament Supremacy," *Inside Kung-fu* **14** (9): 40–44 (September 1987).

However, weight training for body building is not merely a matter of doing near maximal weights explosively, but also a matter of giving variable stress to the muscles. It has been observed by champion power lifters that an excellent growth formula for each body part is: a) three sets near maximal weight, done explosively; b) three sets of medium weight, done rhythmically to failure; and c) three sets of light weight, done with slow, sustained tension and possibly a few negative repetitions to burn out on. Nautilus literature stresses that the greatest gains in strength are produced with one set of repetitions of a weight exercise, performed to failure. In my opinion, a much higher intensity of training is needed than this. For other ideas concerning this, see: J.M. Everson and F. Nagle, "Variable Resistance vs. Isotonic Weight Training in Monozygotic Male Twins," in J. Everson, *The All Sports Training Manual* (Wisconsin: Exercise Consulting Services, 1983), pp. 11–18. Recently Arthur Jones has recanted his famous one-step-to-failure principle and has recognized that specific individuals respond to the same exercise routine differently with respect to range of movement, recovery rate, and strength gains; see F. Hatfield, "Arthur Jones' Latest Discoveries," *Muscle and Fitness* **48** (8);120, 246 (August 1987); and G. Elder, "Arthur Jones' Latest "Discoveries," *Muscle and Fitness* **48** (8): 121, 236–37 (August 1987).

3.   Exercise must be brief and intense. It is physiologically impossible to train at full intensity for long periods of time. In other words, the quality of training is more important than the quantity of training.

4.   There must be in general at least 48 hours of rest between high-intensity workouts, with no more than 96 hours before the next workout, although again there is individual specificity of response with respect to recovery times. This rest period refers only to high-intensity weight training or other strength exercises such as uphill running. Moderate-intensity training in martial-arts skills is fine during a rest period. Split routines are a mistake because of what E. Darden calls the "indirect effect." (See also C.R. Meyers, "Effects of Two Isometric Routines on Strength, Size, and Endurance in Exercised and Non-exercised Arms," *Research Quarterly* **38**:430–40 (1967). When one muscle grows in response to overload, say by heavy squats, then the entire muscle structure of the body also grows, including muscles not directly exercised. The indirect effect is dependent upon the size of the muscle exercised: the larger the muscle, the greater the indirect effect. The body thus

has a blocking device to prevent marked disproportionate growth. But the martial-arts student still needs a balanced training program to strengthen both the upper and lower body.

3. FLEXIBILITY TRAINING

Flexibility may be defined as the range of movement of a body part in or around a joint. Flexibility of the body can be developed to an impressive degree by scientific stretching. There are many advantages that a flexible body offers to a martial-arts practitioner: 1) greater range of movement, which means that kicks can be higher, since flexibility increases the extensibility of the muscles; 2) greater gains in strength, speed, and endurance, especially an increase in punching power, as a muscle will contract more forcibly if a stretch is applied immediately to it before it is contracted; 3) improvements in agility and kinesthetic proficiency; 4) prevention of injuries, since relaxed, flexible muscles are less prone to pulls and tears; 5) improved co-ordination between muscle groups; 6) improved relaxation of muscles; and 7) decrease in muscle tightening after activity. Training for flexibility is therefore of great importance for students of the martial arts, but how does one efficiently train for flexibility? How can substantial gains be made in a relatively short amount of time?

There are three commonly practiced stretching methods used in sports today that I shall now briefly describe.

Rhythmic Stretching Exercises. These stretches involve swinging and rotational exercises to promote a smoothness of movement of the body parts worked. This sort of exercise includes leg swinging in a variety of directions, arm swinging to loosen up the shoulder muscles and joints, trunk rotation, and neck rotation. This is a dynamic form of stretching that is used extensively in dance training. It can yield substantial gains in flexibility over time, but it has its limits as a method of stretching. First, there is a significant danger of muscle tears and injuries to connective tissue if the student does not adequately warm up. Second, this method is limited, as not all important muscles in the body can be fully stretched in this way.

Static Flexibility Exercises.   These movements involve maintaining a fixed stretch, without ballistic stretching (bouncing up and down) for a certain period of time. This method of stretching is fully discussed in: B. Anderson, *Stretching* (California: Shelter Publications, 1984).

Resistive Flexibility Exercises.   This type of stretching involves stretching against varying degrees of resistance supplied by a partner. L.E. Holt, in *Scientific Stretching for Sport* (Halifax: Dalhousie University Press, 1974), described a method of resistive stretching that I believe is the key to martial-arts flexibility. The method is known as proprioceptive neuromuscular facilitation (PNF). An example of how good this method is can be seen by improvements in back flexion, measured by a sit and reach test. It was found that there was up to 200% improvement in just over three months with test subjects (see G. Egger and N. Champion, eds., *The New Fitness Leader's Handbook* [Ken Hurt, Australia: Kangaroo Press, 1986], p. 83). Whether or not substantial gains can be made by advanced stretchers remains to be seen. Nevertheless, this method is well worth practicing by martial-arts students who seem unable to push their flexibility past a sticking point.

PNF involves a static stretch followed by an isometric contraction of a muscle against some source of immovable resistance, such as a training partner. Hold the isometric contraction for about six seconds, then attempt to stretch further. Consider for example a PNF stretch of the adductor-groin area. Perform a stretch with legs straight and spread as widely apart as possible, with a partner (who is sitting in a similar fashion) with his feet on your knees holding them apart. Stretch into a forward bend until you feel a lot of tension. Then squeeze your legs together against your partner's feet. Do not allow any movement for six seconds. Relax, then re-stretch further and repeat PNF.

In Wing Chun kung-fu, a great emphasis is placed upon training that keeps the elbow in line with the center-line. PNF is of use here, and from my practice has produced substantial improvements in the *chi sao* of students. I would like to conclude this section with a description of some important exercises for succesful *chi sao*.

1.   Fully extend your arms in front of you. First attempt to touch the lower forearms together without shrugging the shoulders. Then

perform PNF. When you are flexible enough to touch both elbows together, have a partner stretch your arms so that ultimately the left elbow touches the right side of the chest and the right elbow touches the left side of the chest, keeping the arms straight to make the exercise more difficult. Be certain to use PNF at each stage of your stretching.

2.   Use PNF stretches to increase wrist flexibility. Wrist flexibility and strength is one of the most neglected aspects of martial-arts training. Sticky-hand fighting using Wing Chun's *Bil Jee* techniques requires a high degree of wrist flexibility to enable the striking fingers to dart around guards and attack the throat. The student is advised to perform all standard wrist exercises with PNF. Contracting the wrist muscles against the resistance supplied by a training partner is also an excellent way of building up wrist strength.

4. SPEED AND PLYOMETRIC TRAINING

Many martial artists with a background in physiology are genetic determinists about speed-related activities in martial-art practice. They point out that there are two types of muscle fibers: fast-twitch (FT) and slow-twitch (ST). It is said that the fast-twitch fibers are physiologically suited for high-intensity, short-duration activities such as sprinting, while the slow-twitch fibers have a high aerobic capacity and low anaerobic capacity suited for endurance exercise. Our muscles contain a mixture of each fiber type, the ratio varying from individual to individual. The ratio of FT to ST fibers is said to be genetically fixed and incapable of being influenced by training.

It would be a mistake to conclude, however, that it is impossible to improve speed or that a person with relatively few FT fibers is necessarily slow. The bio-mechanical scientist John P. Kalas in his essay "Fast-Twitch, Slow-Twitch Muscle Fibers: What is the Truth?" (in James A. Peterson, ed., *Total Fitness the Nautilus Way* [New York: Leisure Press, 1978], pp. 201–11), has argued that there is no clear-cut distinction between fast-twitch (white) and slow-twitch (red) muscle fibers in humans. He believes that performing fast exercises for fast muscles and slow exercises for slow muscles is therefore nonsense. Apart from this, it is well known that there is great individual variance for speed and respective FT/ST fiber ratios. An elite marathon runner and a sprinter have been known to have approximately the same percentage of FT and ST fibers. In any case, genetics places only a limit upon an individual's maximum potential for speed and no athletes have ever reached their ultimate potential. There are also technical limitations to the muscle biopsy method, used originally to empirically support the FT/ST distinction (see R.B. Armstrong, et al., "Differential Inter- and Intra-Muscular Responses to Exercise: Considerations in the Use of the Biopsy Technique," in H.G. Knuttgen, J.A. Vogel, and J. Poortmans, eds., *Biochemistry of Exercise* [Champaign, IL: Human Kinetics Publishers, 1983), pp. 775–80).

Speed in executing martial-arts techniques can be improved by training—it is therefore a skill. It is not clear, though, how one can train for speed, and many myths circulate that do more harm than good. The way it can be done is by improving your skill in various areas of force application, such as the quantity of force applied, the direction in which the force is applied, the duration of the application of the force, and the point at which the force is applied. Speed training, therefore, involves applying strength through the full range of motion of the various body parts and then correctly applying force to perform specific skills. Speed training, in short, is an extension of skill coordination, strength, and flexibility training. If you want to be faster follow these rules:

1. Understand your skills; be fully coordinated.
2. Break these skills down into basic movement patterns and perform flexibility and strength exercises for the body parts involved. Remember: speed training is specific, there is no necessary transfer between hand and leg speed-acquisitions. Further, strength exercises do not have to be done fast: what is usually done here is joint damage due to the acceleration of heavy weights rather than any 'serious improvement in speed. The strength-training exercises require working with heavy weights rather than with light weights, using compensatory acceleration. There is an added complication to this principle concerned with plyometric training.
3. Set yourself speed goals. Time your personal rate of punching or kicking on the bags per second—either electronically or slightly less accurately by counting the total number of punches and kicks delivered in a ten second time period. Keep

trying to constantly improve on this record. The same method of training can also be done with defensive hand moves such as the *pak sao* or parry.

I have previously discussed the idea of strength, or absolute strength: the maximum force that can be produced by a subject in movement. There are, however, types of strength. Strength endurance is the ability to exhibit maximum or near maximum effort without a substantial diminishing of force over a time period. A martial-arts student wishes to be able to kick and punch as hard in the closing stages of a fight as he did in the opening stages of the fight. Starting strength is the ability to instantaneously utilize as much muscle fiber as possible in initiating a movement. Explosive strength is the ability to maintain this initial muscular contraction over a distance against opposing forces or resistance. While absolute strength influences both strength endurance, speed strength, and explosive strength, training for these latter forms of strength requires a different strategy from performing a simple weight-lifting program.

One way in which one can develop these other forms of strength is through the Soviet method of plyometrics (see M. Yessis and F. Hatfield, *Plyometric Training* [California: Fitness systems, 1986]; and J. Radcliffe and R. Farentinas, *Plyometrics: Explosive Power Training* [Champaign, IL: Human Kinetics Publishers, Inc., 1985]). Plyometric training is only for the very strong athlete—before attempting it, you must (in the case of the legs) be able to squat at least two and a half times your body weight. For further cautions, see H. Young, "Bowing to the Soviet Myth", *Strength Athlete,* No. 239, 1987, April-May, pp. 11–13. The principle employed here is to get a strong eccentric contraction (or "negative"—the stretching phase of muscle action) and then convert it into a concentric contraction as quickly as possible. Rather than dwell on technical matters it is best to see what a plyometric training program actually looks like. There are four basic plyometric exercises: 1) exercises with weights; 2) jumping exercises; 3) the hit (shock) method; and 4) the use of specialized equipment. Here I will list a few simple plyometric arm and leg exercises for students of the martial arts:

1.   To develop speed in the legs: perform a squat, stopping in the bottom position. Hold for four to five seconds, then leap as high and as quickly as possible. When this exercise becomes easy, hold some

weights. The same type of exercise can be done to develop explosive punches. Lie on a narrow bench with dumbbells almost touching your chest. Hold for four to five seconds, then perform a dumbbell press as fast as possible. Repeat until exhausted. (The same arm exercises can be done without weights by doing explosive push-ups.)

2.   Altitude jumps involve stepping off from various heights so that the muscles of the leg are stretched and undergo maximal eccentric tension, this tension being far greater than the force that can be generated by conscious weight lifting. Begin jumps from two to three feet; advanced athletes may jump from a height of six to seven feet. In doing these jumps think of safety—land only on soft surfaces to prevent joint injuries and don't jump from a height that is beyond your abilities.

3.   Depth jumps can also be done for the arms. Begin in a push-up position with your hands on a block. Push off and drop down from the block, then jump back up to the block. Explosiveness can also be developed in the arms by catching a heavy medicine ball, and throwing it back as fast as possible.

5. AEROBIC AND ANAEROBIC TRAINING

Another important form of conditioning in the martial arts is physiological conditioning or the training of the physiologically effective use of energy. Energy is the capacity to perform work. In the human body, adenosine triphosphate (ATP) is stored in muscle cells and is the immediately usable type of chemical energy for muscular activity. Energy is released from the breakdown of the high-energy bonds of the two phosphate groups in ATP. These chemical reactions are classified as being aerobic or anaerobic, aerobic referring to the presence of oxygen, and anaerobic being a metabolic reaction occurring without the presence of oxygen.

There are three energy systems in the body. The first is the phosphagen system or ATP–PC series, where PC is the energy rich phosphate compound phosphocreatine. This system gives a rapid availability of energy but only a limited amount—0.3 mole in females and 0.6 mole in males. Activities requiring only a few seconds to complete depend upon ATP and PC. The second system is the lactic-acid, or anaerobic, glycolysis system. Here, the breakdown of glycogen anaerobically to lactic acid occurs. The result of this is the production of lactic acid in muscles and blood, which causes muscle fatigue. This system is used for maximum exercise rate between one and three minutes. The third system is the oxygen, or aerobic, system. Here, ATP resynthesis occurs within the mitochondria of the muscle cell by the aerobic breakdown of carbohydrates, fats, and proteins—while the other energy systems are restricted to simple carbohydrates as fuel. There are no fatiguing by-products of this system. VO_2 is the volume of oxygen consumed per minute. The $VO_{2\,max}$ is the maximal volume of oxygen consumed per minute and serves as a measure of the functional power capabilities of the aerobic system of the body.

Martial arts are about 50% aerobic and 50% anaerobic. This means that both energy systems must be trained, because practitioners require both cardiovascular pulmonary endurance as well as the capacity to perform short explosive activities. Skill is of little use without endurance: on the street there are no time-out periods.

Both aerobic and anaerobic types of training should also use the method of progressive overload to provoke adaptive responses. The best way of doing this is by actually practicing the art because of what boxers call the broken rhythm of fighting. Running and sprinting are important and must not be neglected, but a more systematic form of conditioning is needed because endurance in running does not necessarily mean that you will have endurance in punching and sparring. There are other ways of training for both aerobic and anaerobic fitness which are now listed:

1. *Continous Training* for 15 minutes to one hour or more, to get your heart beat to 80–85% of maximum. This is aerobic in nature. Some martial-arts applications include continuous sparring, fighting one person after another until you are defeated by fatigue. This is an excellent way of pushing oneself to one's limits, because the tension of facing an aggressive attacker forces you to overcome tiredness. Sparring is the best form of endurance training for the martial arts.

Sparring of course does not need to be full contact to successfully condition the aerobic (or anaerobic) system(s): non-contact sparring is just as good. The most important thing is that one practices footwork and then launches fast and realistic attacks.

2. *Fartlek Training* is done by adding short intervals of fast work during continuous training lasting for five to ten seconds every two

or three minutes for 30 minutes. An example of this would be five to ten seconds of flat-out punching on the speed bag done between longer intervals of shadow boxing or mirror sparring. There are many other types of explosive activities that could also be practiced to develop anaerobic fitness: these include jumping, running, fast skipping, push ups, fast punching and kicking in the water, the fast lifting of light safe weights, and many gymnastics exercises. Once readers are able to grasp the principles involved, they can make up their own exercises.

I believe that if you train hard in all of the Wing Chun techniques, work out on the speed bag and heavy bag, do your daily road work (running) and spar a lot, you will soon be in top condition. Be sure to continue this training with a balanced diet, low in fat and salt and high in fiber, fresh vegetables, and water. On nutrition for sports, see: T. Kimber, et al., *Gold Gym Nutrition Bible* (Chicago: Contemporary Books, 1986); and for a detailed scientific study, consult magazines and journals such as: *Annual Review of Nutrition, Nutrition Abstracts and Reviews, Nutrition Reviews,* and *Journal of Nutrition.*

Also, if you are really serious about your fitness don't smoke and don't train in rooms polluted by cigarette smoke.

Conclusion

In this book, I have given a logical and scientific description of the three empty-hand forms of Wing Chun kung-fu. I have attempted to go beyond the traditional approach to the writing of martial-arts books, which is secretive (withholding information) and acritical, assuming that a technique is a good one merely because it has been practiced in the past. I have attempted to show why various bodily movements occur in the Wing Chun system, what their meaning is, and how and why they work in the light of biomechanical theory.

In the second volume of this series, *Fighting and Grappling,* I shall give a comprehensive discussion of techniques derived from the *Sil Lum Tao, Chum Kil,* and *Bil Jee* forms. This will include single and double sticky-hands, sticky-legs, grappling (or *chin-na*), throwing techniques, and the so-called poison touch—or *dar mak,* vital strikes to the weak points of the human anatomy. I shall also make the radical, but scientific move of suggesting ways in which the Wing Chun system can be improved.

In the third and final volume of my guide to the complete Wing Chun system, I shall discuss and photographically illustrate the wooden-dummy set, the well-known Wing Chun weapons—the butterfly knives, the six-and-a-half (not feet or inches!) pole set, and the lesser known throwing weapons. In it, the chapter discussions are brief, because differences among the Wing Chun styles in these forms is largely a difference in the organization of the forms or katas, rather than in the assembled techniques.

I do not regard martial-arts systems as fixed, immutable entities given to us by kind gods; on the contrary, the martial arts are human socio-cultural products that can and do change over time in the light of new ideas, experiences, and scientific discoveries about the nature of humankind. In these books I spend considerable time in textual discussion dealing with martial-arts controversies and cleaning up conceptual messes and confusions.

It is my aim to show, that in the age of the gun, the Wing Chun weapons are still relevant—not only as weapons in themselves, but because of many physical benefits derived from training with them.

Glossary

bil jee   One of the most useful hand strikes in Wing Chun, it is featured in the set form of the same name (*see next entry*).

Bil Jee   The thrusting-fingers form, which was traditionally taught only to the most trusted students.

bong sao   One of the most important hand movements in Wing Chun; a bent-elbow hand formation, such that the blade of the hand faces upward.

chi (Pek: *ch'i, qi*)   Actually meaning breath, *chi* is used to describe the intrinsic psycho-physical energy used in the internal arts.

chi gerk   Wing Chun's sticky-leg attacks.

Chi Kung (Pek: *ch'i kung, qigong*)   A type of training to obtain an inner harmony of the body and spirit. It is becoming well known in the West as a method to develop one's internal psychic energy.

Chil Ying   The name of the well-known, front-facing fighting position, in which the fighter stands in parallel stance (see *Kim Nur Mar*).

chin-na   The grappling moves of Wing Chun.

chi sao   The Wing Chun sticky-hand techniques.

Chum Kil   The bridging the gap form of Wing Chun, which introduces three kicks into the Wing Chun system.

ding   An upward-lifting wrist movement used in Wing Chun, not so much as a block but to open up an opponent's guard.

Dit dat jow   A herbal medicine whose name means warm-strike-wine, which is used to prevent arthritis, to heal bruises, to toughen the skin of striking surfaces, and to relieve the pain that results either from over-training or from sustaining a contact injury.

fook sao   The hooking, lying-on-top, hand typically used to redirect attacks.

Futshan Pai   A Wing Chun association located in mainland China, in Futshan, where Wing Chun was originated in the 18th century by a nun and herbal physician named Ng Mui. The name is now also used to describe the style taught in Futshan.

gaun sao   A Wing Chun cross-arm block that completely protects the upper body.

ging (ching)   Inch-force; an immense inner power that can be utilized against an opponent at close range for an explosive shock-wave effect.

gum sao   A Wing Chun push-down block that pushes an opponent's kick away from the body.

haun sao   A wrist-rotating movement, used to twist around guards, or to open up a guard.

jut sao   A sudden downward jerk with the edge of the heel of the hand, to clear a pathway for a strike.

Kim Nur Mar   The Wing Chun parallel stance, in which the fighter stands such that both knees and toes point inward toward the median axis of the body.

kung   Extraordinary intrinsic force that can be tapped into and used after proper development through years of intense kung-fu (*chi kung*) training.

kung-fu   Originally, a Chinese term that meant simply an intense concentration of energy. Later, through popularization of the styles, it came to be synonymous with Chinese martial arts, especially those of the Shaolin lineage.

la   The drawing-down hand of Wing Chun.

Muay Thai   Thai kick-boxing.

pak sao   A defensive parry.

Sil Lum Tao   The first form of the Wing Chun system, the name
   means the Way of the Small Thought. (It is sometimes seen
   written as *Shil Lim Tao.*)
Som Kwok Bo   The correct fighting stance of Wing Chun, a side-on
   pose with the forward foot turned slightly in and the back foot
   held at 45 degrees to the median line of the body.

t'an-tien (Cant: *tandim*)   According to traditional Chinese theory, an
   area of the body located about three inches beneath the navel
   and another two inches within the body; the psychic or energy
   center akin to a Yogic chakra, which produces and stores the vital
   energy (*chi*) of the body. This energy can be directed against an
   opponent with the proper training.
taun sao   The asking-hand of Wing Chun, a straight thrusting-hand
   move used to deflect punches.
til sao   A defensive lifting deflection designed for counter-attacking
   a punch with a grappling hand move.
tor sao   The Wing Chun *tor sao* is really a modified *fook sao* with the
   fingers facing downward.

Wing Chun / Wing Tsun   A non-traditional Chinese martial art that
   is highly regarded as an effective self-defense system. It is said to
   have been invented by a nun named Ng Mui, one of the only five
   survivors of the total destruction of the original Shaolin Temple.
   Legend has it that Ng Mui traveled to Futshan province, where
   she developed her own fighting style and passed it on to her best
   disciple, the daughter of another student, bean-curd maker Yim
   San Sohk, whose given name was Wing Chun (Beautiful Spring).
wu sao   A defensive hand move known as worshiping the Buddha.

yin/yang   According to Chinese cosmology, the two basic principles of the universe, which are both opposite to each other but
   complementary at the same time. Yang is characterised by things
   that are positive, active, and male; yin, by things that are negative,
   passive, and female.